THE COST OF DOING BU$INESS STUDY, 2025 EDITION

NAHB®
National Association of Home Builders

The Cost of Doing Business Study, 2025 Edition

BuilderBooks, a Service of the National Association of Home Builders (NAHB)

Patricia Potts	Senior Director, Publisher
Joe Rudden	Cover Design
Robert Brown	Composition

Jim Tobin	NAHB Chief Executive Officer
Robert Dietz	Senior Vice President and Chief Economist, Economics and Housing Policy
Paul Emrath	Vice President, Economics and Housing Policy
Rose Quint	Assistant Vice President, Survey Research, Economics and Housing Policy
Marcia Childs	Director, Business Management Department

Published in the United States of America

28 27 26 25 1 2 3 4 5

ISBN-13: 978-0-86718-823-3
eISBN-13: 978-0-86718-824-0

For further information, please contact:
National Association of Home Builders
1201 15th Street, NW
Washington, DC 20005-2800
BuilderBooks.com

Contents

Figures

Chapter 1. All Survey Respondents

Chapter 2. Builders with Land Costs

Chapter 3. Builders without Land Costs

Chapter 4. Combination Builders

Chapter 5. Small-Volume Builders

Chapter 6. Production Builders

Chapter 7. Builder Financial Performance by Region and Business Model

Chapter 8. Operations

Chapter 9. Historical Data and Trends

Tables

Chapter 1. All Survey Respondents

Chapter 2. Builders with Land Costs

Chapter 3. Builders without Land Costs

Chapter 4. Combination Builders

Chapter 5. Small-Volume Builders

Chapter 6. Production Builders

Chapter 9. Historical Data and Trends

Acknowledgments

The NAHB Economics and Housing Policy Group conducted the survey and tabulated the findings. The NAHB Business Management and Information Technology Committee provided oversight since it has jurisdiction over matters relating to improving the business management skills of NAHB's builder members in order to enhance their competitiveness, profitability, and professionalism.

In accordance with the NAHB strategic plan objectives, the committee makes policy recommendations on business management issues, develops educational programs, writes and publishes manuals, conducts business management research, and provides consulting assistance to other committees

The Committee's mission statement is

> *"To serve as the leading resource to the building industry in the areas of management, finance, information technology, operations, and human resources"*

Members of the 2024 Business Management & Information Technology Committee

John Atlee, Water Doctors

Dianne Beaton, CAPS, CGA, 2DiFore Marketing Solutions LLC

Vince Butler, CAPS, CGR, GMB, GMR, Butler Brothers Corp.

Cynthia Cepko, CMP, CSP, Master CSP, MIRM, Granite Homes Property Management

Amanda Corle, EOC Liaison, Ketchum Tile

Darylene Dennon, Solid Energy, Inc.

Rebecca Gamble, Hall Quality Homes

John Hodgin, CAPS, John Hodgin Construction Co., Inc.

John Jones, SoftPlan Systems Inc.

Erin LeCorgne, Draper & Kramer Mortgage Corp.

Chuck Miller, CAPS, CGB, CGP, CGR, CMP, CSP, GMB, GMR, Master CGP, Master CSP, MIRM, Chuck Miller Consulting LLC

Russ Pies, Builders FirstSource

Owen Shigley, Shigley Construction Co., Inc.

Cory Sillars, Dan Sillars General Contractor, Inc.

We also thank the following contributing writers and reviewers:

Joyce Duerfeldt, Nationwide Contractors' Alliance Inc.

Alan Hanbury Jr., CAPS, CGP, CGR, GMR

Steven W. Hays, Sr., CPA, RubinBrown, LLC

Carrie Roeger, White Stone Residential, LLC

We also thank the following contributing writers and reviewers:

Vince Butler, GMB, GMR, CAPS, Butler Brothers Corporation

David O'Brien, CPA, CGMA, Mosley Glick O' Brien, Inc.

We thank those builders who provided their valuable financial information for this 21st edition in *The Cost of Doing Business Study* series. Without their time and effort, this study would not have been possible

Introduction

Although competent management and sharp technical skills are essential for the long-term success of a company, they alone don't determine the economic viability of a business. The industry environment in which it operates is also of paramount significance for the financial performance of any company. Factors such as the number and size of its competitors, barriers to entry or exit, capital requirements, labor availability, economies of scale, or the bargaining power of customers and suppliers all play a role in the potential profitability of a company. In this macro context, one of the most useful strategies to evaluate a company's competitiveness is to compare its financial performance against profitability benchmarks for the entire industry. For this reason, the National Association of Home Builders periodically conducts the Cost of Doing Business Study – a nationwide survey of single-family home-building companies designed to produce profitability benchmarks for the industry.

The Cost of Doing Business Study provides information that will help you with resource allocation, budgeting, and target setting for various costs and expense lines. More broadly, the study can help you create an overall strategy to achieve higher financial results. By providing recent and reliable data on industrywide profit margins and financial ratios, the study helps builders remain (or become) successful in today's competitive environment.

How the Study was Prepared

The Cost of Doing Business Study survey questionnaire was sent electronically to more than 8,000 companies in April 2024. The questionnaire asked for 2023 financial and operational information, and details about the type of single-family units closed in 2023. The analysis presented in *The Cost of Doing Business Study* is based only on responses from builders who reported their main operation to be single-family production or custom home building (either on owners' or builders' lots). NAHB received 485 partial or complete responses—

not every question was answered by all respondents. Survey responses are categorically confidential and at no point is any company-specific information revealed. Only aggregate calculations are published, and survey respondents remain anonymous.

Organization of the Study

Nine chapters of study results and two related appendices comprise *The Cost of Doing Business Study, 2025 Edition.* The study is organized as follows:

Chapters 1–6 provide detailed information on gross profit, net profit, assets, liabilities, owner's equity, and financial ratios. Chapter 1 provides aggregated information for all survey respondents, including a comparison between the top 25% and bottom 25% of builders. Subsequent chapters present the data for specific types of companies, such as small-volume and production builders.

Chapter 7 compares builders' performance by geographic region and business model (builders with land cost, without land cost, and combination builders). Chapter 8 provides data about the main operation of respondents, years in business, and the number of units closed in 2023. Chapter 9 discusses historical trends based on data from *The Cost of Doing Business Study,* NAHB Construction Costs surveys, and financial data that are available from the largest 15 public builders.

How to Use the Study

The Cost of Doing Business Study contains a wealth of information about the residential construction industry, but it is much more than a statistical report. Builders can use the study as a benchmark for their businesses by comparing their net profit to the industry average, or better yet, to the top most profitable quartile. A company's ability to consistently generate adequate net profit strongly influences whether it will be successful in the long run.

By aggregating earnings information in the home building industry, the study allows builders to analyze their financial performance, determine whether they are optimally managing their business, and assess whether they are achieving their business goals. The study helps company owners pinpoint areas for improvement, set budget targets, and create a road map for boosting profitability and increasing efficiency. The study breaks down survey findings by region, 2023 revenue, number of units closed, and whether builders have land costs. Where applicable, the study shows results for the top and bottom quartiles (in terms of net profit performance). It also shows the average performance for all builders within a size category, i.e., small (1 to 25 closings) vs. production (26+ closings) builders. In addition, the study compares results from the most recent survey (2023 fiscal year data) with the previous two surveys (2017 and 2020 data).

To get maximum value from this study, gather your financial information, including your income statement and balance sheet, and see how your performance compares with other builders. Once you compare your company's performance against the aggregate for similar builders, you can use the findings to make business decisions and influence the behavior of others who directly impact your company's success. For example, you can use the study as a selling point to lenders. If your company performs better than or even at the same level as the industry average, present these facts to negotiate better loan terms or interest rates. Results can also help motivate your employees, by using industry averages as the basic performance level for rewarding employees with merit increases or bonuses.

Industry Profitability

On average, single-family builders reported higher gross and net profit margins in 2023 than in 2020. Their average 8.7% net profit margin was the highest in more than three decades and second only to the series peak of 10.0% in 1991.

- The average gross profit margin increased from 18.2% in 2020 to 20.7% in 2023.
- The average net profit margin rose from 7.0% to 8.7% during this period.

Gross profit equals sales minus the *cost of sales*. Cost of sales comprises:

- Materials and labor used in a home's construction.
- Land on which the home is built.
- Indirect construction costs (field or construction expenses) that cannot be tied to a specific home.

Gross profit is measured before deducting operating expenses (financing, sales and marketing, general and administrative, depreciation, and owner's compensation). Here's how to calculate gross profit as a percentage of revenue:

1. Subtract the cost of sales from total sales (revenue).
2. Divide that gross profit by total sales (revenue).

The following example calculates the gross profit margin for a company with $2 million in total sales (revenue) and $1.4 million in cost of sales.

$2 million – $1.4 million = $600,000

$600,000 ÷ $2 million = 0.30 or 30%

You can (and should) calculate gross profit at all operational levels—by home, by community, and for all jobs over the year.

Net profit is the income from sales after deducting the cost of sales and expenses, including owner's compensation. In other words, net profit is the money a business earns after it has paid all the costs of both the project (hard costs) and the operating expenses (soft costs). When comparing your net profits with the overall industry performance, it is best to consider the pretax net profits because many factors (not discussed in this study) determine the taxes a business pays.

Consider the same company in which total sales are $2 million; *cost of sales,* or cost of goods sold, is $1.4 million; and operating expenses plus owner's compensation total $400,000. As described earlier, the gross profit is $600,000, a *gross margin* of 30%. Operating expenses take up 20% of total sales, leaving a net profit of $200,000 and a net profit margin of 10%. To calculate the net profit as a percentage of sales, subtract the cost of sales, operating expenses, and owner's compensation from total sales, and then divide that net profit by total sales as follows:

$2 million – $1.4 million – $400,000 = $200,000

$200,000 ÷ $2 million = .1 or 10%

Applying the Information to Your Business

What is an acceptable profit margin? While there isn't an ideal number, industry experts suggest aiming for gross profit margins of 22 to 27% and net profits of 8 to15%. Although many companies post higher numbers, others do not achieve these levels. The averages presented in *The Cost of Doing Business Study* aren't necessarily appropriate goals for every company. To determine your profit goals, consider your level of risk, the cyclical nature of the industry, and the return you could get for your capital if you invested it in another business sector or in a money market account.

Be cautious when considering changing your business plan based on information in this publication. Consider not only the benefits of the proposed change, but its costs. For example, although you could raise your home sales price to increase your profit margin that is not a sustainable strategy for growing your bottom line. Because your homes probably would be too expensive for the market, your sales velocity would slow or stop.

Although *The Cost of Doing Business Study* is an essential resource to help you manage your business more effectively and profitably, you need other tools as well. These include your annual operating budget, which you can use to evaluate monthly financial performance. You also need tools to monitor construction quality, employee or trade contractor performance, schedules, and pre- and post-construction systems. When you measure performance in essential areas, you will have the information needed to improve management, quality, and profitability.

1

All Survey Respondents

Although competent management and sharp technical skills are essential for long-term company success, they alone do not determine the economic viability of a business. The industry environment in which it operates is also of paramount significance for the financial performance of any company. Factors such as the number and size of its competitors, barriers to entry or exit, capital requirements, labor availability, economies of scale, or the bargaining power of customers and suppliers all play a role in the potential profitability of a company. In this macro context, one of the most useful strategies to evaluate a company's competitiveness is to compare its financial performance against profitability benchmarks for the entire industry. For this reason, the National Association of Home Builders periodically conducts *The Cost of Doing Business Study* — a nationwide survey of single-family home-building companies designed to produce profitability benchmarks for the industry.

More than 8,000 builder members received the online survey in April 2024, confidentially requesting the income statement and balance sheet for their companies for fiscal year 2023. The sample was stratified to accurately represent builders across the four Census regions of the country and across builder size categories (in terms of the number of single-family units built). In total, 485 responses were received, but not all questions were answered by every respondent.

The financial analysis presented throughout *The Cost of Doing Business Study* is based solely on responses from builders who reported their main operation as single-family home building, whether production or custom (on the owner's or builder's lots). Table 1.1 breaks down the responses by U.S. Census region, type of builder, number of single-family homes closed in 2023, and total 2023 revenue.[1]

---

[1] Due to rounding, the numbers in the tables presented throughout the study may not add up to 100%.

Table 1.1. Respondents' profile

	% of total
Region	
Northeast: Connecticut, Maine, Massachusetts, New Hampshire, New Jersey, New York, Pennsylvania, Rhode Island, Vermont	7
Midwest: Illinois, Indiana, Iowa, Kansas, Michigan, Minnesota, Missouri, Nebraska, North Dakota, Ohio, South Dakota, Wisconsin	24
South: Alabama, Arkansas, Delaware, District of Columbia, Florida, Georgia, Kentucky, Louisiana, Maryland, Mississippi, North Carolina, Oklahoma, South Carolina, Tennessee, Texas, Virginia, West Virginia	51
West: Alaska, Arizona, California, Colorado, Hawaii, Idaho, Montana, Nevada, New Mexico, Oregon, Utah, Washington, Wyoming	18
Type of Builder	
With land costs	40
Without land costs	31
Combination	29
Single-family homes closed in 2023	
<10	45
10–25	18
26–99	14
≥100	22
Total 2023 Revenue	
< $2 million	21
$2 to $9.9 million	42
$10 million+	37

Fifty-one percent of the study's respondents operate in the South, 24% are in the Midwest, 18% in the West, and 7% are based in the Northeast. This breakdown reasonably reflects the actual distribution of single-family housing starts across regions in 2023 (South: 60%; West: 22%; Midwest: 12%; and Northeast: 6%).

Looking at the types of builders who responded to the survey reveals that 40% were builders *with land costs* — defined in this study as those who only build speculative or pre-sold homes on lots they own. Another 31% were builders without land costs — defined as those who build exclusively on lots owned by their customers. The remaining 29% were combination builders — defined as those who build homes on their lots and on their customers' lots.

This year's breakdown by type of builder is significantly different from past years. The share of respondents who build without land costs — 31% — is at an all-time high, having jumped from 19% in the previous study. Combination builders are a much smaller share of the respondent pool in 2023 (29%) than in 2020 (46%).

For this study, small-volume builders are those with 25 or fewer closings in 2023, while production builders are those with 26 or more closings. A total of 63% of all respondents were small-volume builders. Within that group, 45% closed fewer than 10 homes and 18% closed 10 to 25 homes. Of the 36% of production builders, 14% closed 26 to 99 units, and 22% closed 100 units or more.

The rest of this chapter provides detailed information on gross profit, net profit, assets, liabilities, owner's equity, and financial ratios aggregated for all builders in the study, including a comparison between the top 25% most successful and the bottom 25% least successful builders (in terms of net margins). Subsequent chapters present the data for specific types of companies, such as small-volume or production builders.

Balance Sheet and Income Statement

The Cost of Doing Business Study survey asked respondents for data from their 2023 income statement, including details about revenue, cost of sales and expenses. On the revenue side, the survey requested information about income generated from building single-family and multifamily homes, as well as from residential remodeling and light commercial/industrial building. For cost of sales, builders were asked to provide land costs and direct and indirect construction costs. Data on operating expenses were requested for financing expenses, sales and marketing expenses, general and administrative expenses, depreciation, and owner's compensation.

In addition to the income statement, the survey also inquired about builders' 2023 balance sheets. More specifically, it asked about how much money was held in cash, how much in receivables and inventories, the amount tied to construction work in progress, the amounts owed in current liabilities, construction loans, and long-term liabilities, and the total amount held as owner's equity.

To provide historical context for the current findings, this study compares the 2023 data with results from previous editions of *The Cost of Doing Business Study,* particularly the last two editions covering fiscal years 2017 and 2020. Before delving into results, it is important to provide a broad overview of the economic conditions builders faced during the year these financial statements were generated. The U.S. economy was resilient in 2023, growing 2.5% and creating over 2.5 million jobs, despite a sustained campaign of interest rate hikes by the Federal Reserve Bank to rein in high inflation. In the summer of 2022, inflation (measured by the Consumer Price Index) hit a four-decade high of 9.1%, buoyed by COVID-era government outlays, supply chain disruptions, and strong consumer spending. Multiple rounds of monetary tightening by the Fed led the 30-year mortgage rate to reach 7.8% in October 2023 and a 6.8% average for the year–the highest since 2001. At the same time, the restrictive monetary policy made credit for new residential construction difficult and expensive, keeping rates on acquisition, development, and construction (AD&C) loans firmly above 10% throughout 2023.

High mortgage rates froze the existing housing market in 2023 as millions of homeowners with mortgage rates below 5% felt 'locked in' their homes and postponed moving. This caused existing home sales to fall to 4.1 million units — 19% lower than in 2022 and the lowest since 1995. On the new home side, expensive credit for buyers and builders drove the latter to start 948,000 single-family homes in 2023, down 6% from 2022 and 16% from 2021.

Housing affordability, meanwhile, has deteriorated sharply in recent years. In addition to mortgage rates not seen in a generation, a large imbalance between housing demand and housing supply gave rise to steep growth in home prices. Between 2020 and 2023, the median price of existing homes jumped 31%, up to $394,100. To a slightly lesser extent, new home prices also rose during this period, up 27% to $428,600. Interestingly, in 2023, a typical new home sold for only 9% more than a typical existing home, a much smaller gap than in 2013, when new homes sold for a 36% premium over existing homes.

Keeping this large context in mind, Table 1.2 shows that total revenue for single-family builders in 2023 averaged $11.3 million–17% lower than in 2020 ($13.7 million) and 31% lower than in 2017 ($16.4 million). The $11.3 million average revenue builders reported in 2023 was 40% lower than the $18.7 million reported in 2006 (the peak in this series), but close to 60% higher than the $7.1 million reported in 2010 (the most recent trough).

Builders spent an average of $9.0 million on the total cost of sales in 2023, which means they spent 79.3% of revenue on land, direct, and indirect costs–1.5 percentage points less than in 2020 (81.8%). Most of the savings came from less spending on land, partially because there were more builders without land costs (31%) than in 2020 (19%). On average, builders spent 8.3% of their revenue on land costs in 2023, compared to 13.0% in 2020. In contrast, and shifting in the opposite direction, the direct costs to build single-family homes (e.g., labor, materials, contractors) increased from 60.1% of revenue in 2020 to 64.0% in 2023.

After subtracting all costs of sales from revenue, builders averaged a gross profit of $2.3 million in 2023, a 20.7% gross margin. That was 1.5 percentage points ahead of 2020's gross margin (18.2%) and the highest in the series since 2006 (20.8%). As a point of reference, at its lowest point during the 2008 housing recession, builders' average gross margin was only 14.4%. For a complete summary of the history of this study, please see Chapter 9.

Table 1.2. Gross profit

	2017		2020		2023	
	Average ($1,000s)	Share of revenue (%)	Average ($1,000s)	Share of revenue (%)	Average ($1,000s)	Share of revenue (%)
Revenue	16,429	100.0	13,702	100.0	11,327	100.0
Cost of sales						
Land costs	2,068	12.6	1,784	13.0	946	8.3
Direct costs: single-family	10,306	62.7	8,242	60.1	7,254	64.0
Direct costs: multifamily, remodeling, light commercial/industrial	425	2.6	685	5.0	393	3.5
Indirect construction costs	469	2.9	384	2.8	338	3.0
Other costs*	42	0.3	118	0.9	52	0.5
Total cost of sales	13,309	81.0	11,212	81.8	8,983	79.3
Gross profit	**3,120**	**19.0**	**2,490**	**18.2**	**2,344**	**20.7**

* This category includes the costs associated with the sale of land (raw or developed), trade-ins, repossessions, investment property rental, parking facilities, and recreational facilities, construction management activities, design

While builders spent a lower share of revenue on the cost of sales in 2023 than in 2020, they spent slightly more on operating expenses — 12.0% vs. 11.2%, respectively (Table 1.3). The change marked the first relative increase in expenses since 2008, when builders spent a steep 17.4% of revenue on operating expenses. Over the following decade, however, rigorous belt-tightening cut this share to 14.7% in 2010, 12.5% in 2012 and 2014, 11.4% in 2017, and to an all-time low of 11.2% in 2020.

The main culprit for the relative growth in operating expenses was an increase in general and administrative expenses, which took up 5.4% of revenue in 2023, up one full percentage point from 2020 (4.4%)[2]. Larger shares of revenue going towards owner's compensation (1.9% in 2023 vs. 1.3% in 2020) and financing expenses (1.6% vs. 1.3%) also contributed to the overall increase in operating expenses. Sales & marketing expenses, on the other hand, continued their long-term downward trend, accounting for only 3.1% of revenue in 2023, compared to 5.4% in 2008, 5.2% (2010), 5.1% (2012), 5.0% (2014), 4.7% (2017), and 4.1% in 2020.

In the end, the drop in cost of sales relative to revenue allowed builders to post an average net profit margin of 8.7% in 2023, up from 7.0% in 2020, and the highest since the series peak of 10.0% in 1991. In the last 15 years, the industry average on net profit margin saw a remarkable recovery, going from an all-time low of -3.0% in 2008 to 8.7% in 2023. Figure 1.1 summarizes builders' income statements for 2023 (Appendix IV.1).

Table 1.3. Net profit

	2017		2020		2023	
	Average ($1,000s)	Share of revenue (%)	Average ($1,000s)	Share of revenue (%)	Average ($1,000s)	Share of revenue (%)
Gross profit	3,120	19.0	2,490	18.2	2,344	20.7
Operating expenses						
Financing expenses	220	1.3	178	1.3	176	1.6
Sales & mktg. expenses	779	4.7	556	4.1	349	3.1
General & administrative expenses	666	4.1	597	4.4	608	5.4
Depreciation	19	0.1	20	0.1	14	0.1
Owner's compensation	194	1.2	180	1.3	211	1.9
Total operating expenses	1,879	11.4	1,531	11.2	1,358	12.0
Net profit (loss)	**1,241**	**7.6**	**959**	**7.0**	**985**	**8.7**

[2] Among other expenses, this line of the income statement includes salaries, benefits, taxes, insurance, and travel, most of which have seen significant price escalation in recent years.

Figure 1.1. Cost of sales, expenses, and net profit (% of revenue)

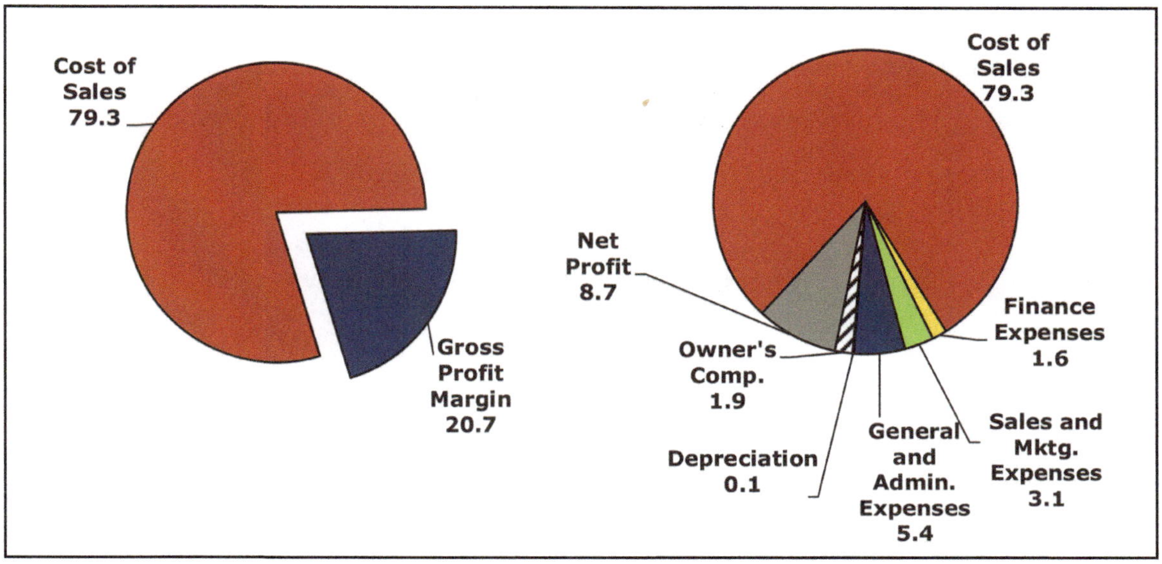

In addition to the income statement, *The Cost of Doing Business Study* has tracked the balance sheet of single-family builders over time. As Table 1.4 shows, builders responding to the survey had total assets averaging $7.2 million in 2023, down about 23% from 2020 ($9.4 million) and 10% from 2017 ($8.0 million)[3]. The average builder held most of its assets as construction work in progress ($4.4 million or 61.3% of all assets), another $494,000 was in receivables and inventories (6.8%), $460,000 in other current assets (6.4%), and $913,000 was tied to other assets (12.6%). Builders also had an average of $929,000 in cash, about 12.9% of their assets, marking the second consecutive time the cash share exceeded 10% (It was 13.1% in 2020.). The latter is an interesting fact because, before 2020, builders had never reported holding more than 8% of their assets in cash in the history of *The Cost of Doing Business Study*.

On the liabilities side, respondents owed an average of $4.5 million in 2023, about 26% less than in 2020 ($6.1 million) and 15% less than in 2017 ($5.3 million). High interest rates on construction loans significantly impacted builders' debt positions. In 2023, for example, only 62.0% of assets were financed through debt, the lowest debt-to-assets ratio in the history of the study. In comparison, debt was the source of financing for 64.3% of assets in 2020, 65.8% in 2017, and — going back further — a much larger 73.7% in 2006!

[3] *The Cost of Doing Business Study* is not designed as a longitudinal survey tracking the same companies over time. Instead, each year's study is based on responses from independent samples of current members of the NAHB

Another consequence of elevated borrowing costs has been a shift away from short-term debt. In 2023, only 44.3% of builders' total assets were financed through current liabilities, which was lower than in 2017 and 2020 (~56%), and the lowest share in the study's history. Instead, builders have gravitated toward long-term liabilities, doubling the share of assets financed through this type of debt from 8.4% in 2020 to 17.7% in 2023.

As builders' overall reliance on debt diminished in 2023, equity took on a larger role. While the absolute amount of invested capital declined from an average of $3.4 million in 2020 to $2.7 million in 2023, the share of assets financed through equity rose from 35.7% to 38.0% — the highest in the history of this series.

Table 1.4. Balance sheet

	2017		2020		2023	
	Average ($1,000s)	Share of total (%)	Average ($1,000s)	Share of total (%)	Average ($1,000s)	Share of total (%)
Assets						
Current assets						
Cash	626	7.8	1,235	13.1	929	12.9
Receivables & inventories	588	7.3	850	9.0	494	6.8
Construction work in progress	5,155	64.2	5,891	62.4	4,428	61.3
Other current assets	907	11.3	571	6.0	460	6.4
Total current assets	7,276	90.6	8,547	90.5	6,312	87.4
Other assets	758	9.4	894	9.5	913	12.6
Total assets	**8,034**	**100.0**	**9,441**	**100.0**	**7,224**	**100.0**
Liabilities						
Current liabilities	1,869	23.3	2,921	30.9	1,150	15.9
Construction loans payable	2,611	32.5	2,356	24.9	2,049	28.4
Total current liabilities	4,480	55.8	5,276	55.9	3,199	44.3
Long-term loans payable	749	9.3	680	7.2	492	6.8
Other long-term liabilities	58	0.7	112	1.2	789	10.9
Total liabilities	**5,287**	**65.8**	**6,068**	**64.3**	**4,479**	**62.0**
Owner's equity	**2,747**	**34.2**	**3,373**	**35.7**	**2,745**	**38.0**
Total liabilities & owner's equity	**8,034**	**100.0**	**9,441**	**100.0**	**7,224**	**100.0**

The current ratio is a liquidity measure that evaluates a company's ability to repay its short-term liabilities using its short-term assets. It is calculated by dividing current assets by current liabilities, and in general, the higher the current ratio the healthier the financial state of a company. In 2023, the current ratio for all single-family home builders responding to the survey was 1.97, or in other words, builders had 97% more current assets than current liabilities (Table 1.5). The ratio was higher than in 2020 (1.62), higher than in 2006 at the peak of the housing boom (1.43), and in fact, is the highest current ratio in the history of the study.

Another important gauge of a company's financial health is its debt-to-equity ratio. Calculated by dividing total liabilities by total equity, this ratio measures the level of leverage, and therefore risk, that exists in a company. In 2023, builders reported the lowest average debt-to-equity ratio in the history of the study, at 1.63. Put simply, that means builders in 2023 were running financially safe operations, where debt was only 63% higher than the capital invested in the business. This is in stark contrast to 2006 conditions when builders' debt-to-equity ratio reached a record 2.80, a signal of the significant levels of risk taken during the housing boom. As a point of reference, a debt-to-equity ratio above 4.0 is considered so risky, that most financial institutions would likely turn down additional borrowing requests from any company with that level of debt.

Two additional ratios, return on assets (ROA) and return on equity (ROE), reveal a company's effectiveness at using its assets and invested capital to churn out profits. In 2023, builders' ROA stood at 13.6%, a higher return than in 2020 (10.2%). The improvement resulted from achieving about the same level of net profits ($959,000 in 2020 vs. $985,000 in 2023) while using far fewer assets ($9.4 million vs. $7.2 million). For similar reasons, obtaining about the same level of net profits while employing far less capital ($3.4 million vs. $2.7 million), builders' ROE was higher in 2023 (35.9%) than in 2020 (28.4%).

Table 1.5. Financial ratios

	2017	2020	2023
Current ratio	1.62	1.62	1.97
Debt-to-equity ratio	1.92	1.80	1.63
Return on assets	15.4%	10.2%	13.6%
Return on equity	45.2%	28.4%	35.9%

Top and Bottom 25%

When looking at profitability benchmarks, it is useful to look at averages across the industry, but it is also important to understand how the most and least successful quartiles of builders performed. Such analysis allows us to see the differences in the cost and expense structures of the most and least profitable groups of builders. With that goal in mind, this section shows results tabulated separately for two cohorts of respondents: those in the top 25% in terms of net profit margins and those in the bottom 25% (Appendix IV.2).

Total revenue among builders in the top 25% group averaged $15.6 million in 2023, 161% more than the $6.0 million averaged among builders in the bottom 25% group. The sources of that revenue differed across the two cohorts of builders: while nearly all the top group's revenue (96.0%) came from single-family home building, the share was only 81.7% for the bottom group. In contrast, residential remodeling was a larger source of revenue for the bottom 25% cohort (10.2%) than for the top 25% cohort (1.0%).

Analyzing total cost of sales side-by-side reveals that the most successful quartile spent significantly less on sales costs (70.3%) of their revenue than the least successful quartile (83.0%). The most important variation occurred in direct construction costs for single-family building, on which the top group spent 56.7% of revenue, compared to 66.7% among the bottom group. After accounting for all costs of sales, the gross profit margin was 29.7% and 17.0%, respectively, for the top and bottom 25% groups (Figure 1.2).

All operating expense lines were lower for the top 25% group (who spent 12.0% of their revenue on them) than for the bottom 25% group (who spent 18.4%). For example, financing expenses were only 1.2% of the top group's revenue, less than half the 2.8% share for the bottom group. And whereas the top performers spent 5.2% on general and administrative expenses, the bottom performers spent 7.5%.

After subtracting all operating expenses from gross profit, the most successful group of builders averaged a net profit margin of 17.7%, a sharp contrast to the -1.4% net margin posted by the least successful group. In this study, it is typical for the bottom 25% group to average negative net profit margins. In fact, since results were first tabulated separately for the top and bottom quartiles in 2002, the latter group has posted negative net profit margins in every iteration of the study except in 2014 (0.9%) and 2017 (1.1%).

In addition to the analysis of margins alone, it is also useful to calculate a broader measure of performance by combining the net profit margin for the company and the share of revenue spent on owner's compensation. Given how blurry the lines can be between the business' profit and compensation for its owner(s) in many (especially, small) companies, this measure paints a more holistic picture of profitability. As Figure 1.2 shows, this broader measure of profitability was 10.6% for all builders combined, 20.1% for the top 25% group, and 2.1% for the bottom 25% group.

Figure 1.2. Profit margins and owner's compensation (% of revenue)

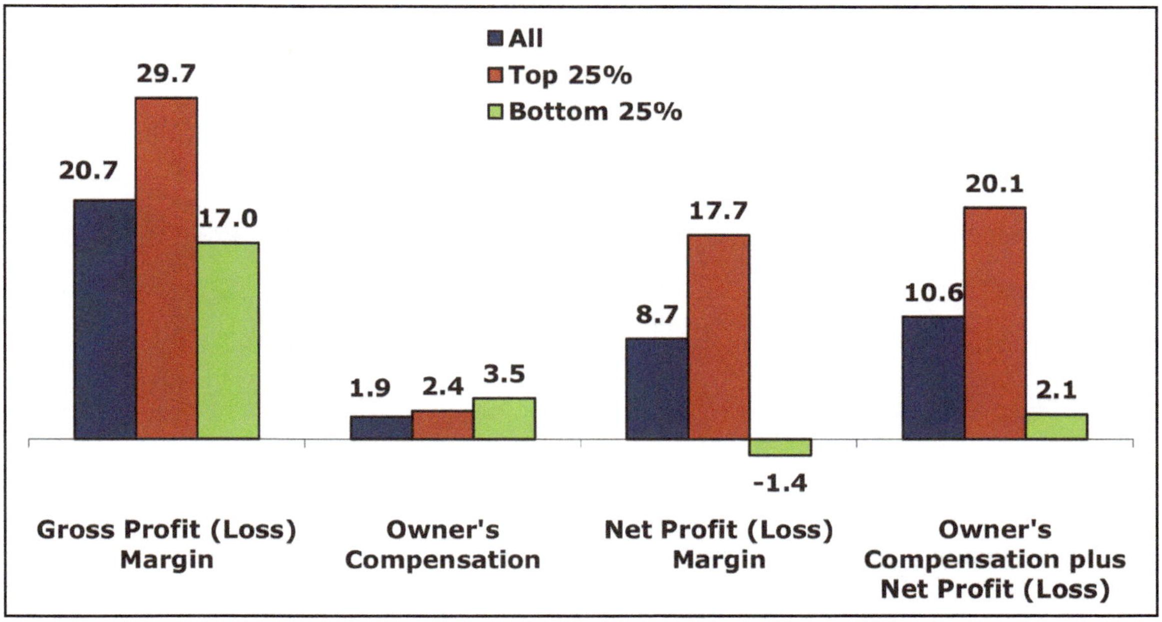

The 2023 balance sheet for the top 25% of respondents shows they had an average of $10.6 million in total assets, $4.1 million in liabilities, and $6.6 million in owner's equity. On the other hand, builders in the bottom 25% had significantly fewer assets ($3.5 million), total liabilities ($3.0 million), and owner's equity ($519,000). Table 1.6 summarizes important statistics from the income statement and balance sheet for the top and bottom 25% of respondents.

Table 1.6. Top and bottom 25%

	2017		2020		2023	
	Top 25%	Bottom 25%	Top 25%	Bottom 25%	Top 25%	Bottom 25%
Gross profit (loss) margin (%)	22.10	13.90	23.70	9.10	29.70	17.00
Net profit (loss) margin (%)	11.40	1.10	12.40	-2.70	17.70	-1.40
Total assets (millions $)	15.97	5.63	8.54	2.48	10.63	3.54
Owner's equity (millions $)	6.61	2.36	3.10	0.32	6.57	0.52
Current ratio	1.84	2.29	2.17	1.22	2.51	1.11
Debt-to-equity ratio	1.41	1.39	1.72	6.65	0.62	5.82
Return on assets (%)	21.10	1.50	23.50	-4.00	25.97	-2.44
Return on equity (%)	50.80	3.50	63.90	-30.70	42.00	-16.63

Results for the most successful group of builders reveal their financial performance continued to improve between 2020 and 2023. Their average gross profit margin increased from 23.7% to 29.7%, while their net margin rose from 12.4% to 17.7%. Lower debt levels coupled with a significant injection of capital deleveraged them, sinking their debt-to-equity ratio below 1.0 (0.62). This group's ROA grew from 23.5% to 25.9% between 2020 and 2023, which means net income was equivalent to about 26% of the assets held in their balance sheets. The group's ROE, meanwhile, was a healthy 42.0% in 2023, lower than in 2020 (63.9%) due to stronger growth in equity than in returns during this period.

The least successful group of builders managed to keep a tighter lid on the total cost of sales in 2023 than in 2020, leading their average gross profit margin to rise from 9.1% to 17.0%. Despite that improvement, much higher operating expenses left them with a net loss of -1.4%, about half the net loss they reported in 2020 (-2.7%). Due to relatively stronger growth in current liabilities than current assets between 2020 and 2023, this group's current ratio slipped back from 1.22 to 1.11; while higher growth in equity vis-à-vis debt led their debt-to-equity ratio to drop from 6.65 to 5.82. Although less painful than in 2020, the ROA and ROE for this group remained in negative territory in 2023, at -2.4% and -16.6%, respectively.

2

Builders With Land Costs

Builders with land costs (those that only build spec or presold homes on their lots) responding to *The Cost of Doing Business Study* averaged $17.9 million in total revenue in 2023, about 26% higher than in 2020 ($14.2 million) and 22% higher than in 2017 ($14.7 million) (Table 2.1). Builders with land costs spent a smaller share of revenue on costs of sales items in 2023 (77.5%) than in 2020 (80.7%) or 2017 (79.1%). The most important change in the cost structure since the last study was a drop in the share of revenue spent on land, which declined from 17.8% to 11.2%[4]. This allowed builders with land costs to report an average gross profit margin of 22.5% in 2023 ($4.0 million), up from 19.3% in 2020 and the group's highest gross margin ever in this series. In previous studies, their gross margin exceeded 20% only three times: in 2004 (22.3%), 2006 (22.1%), and 2017 (20.9%).

Table 2.1. Gross profit

	2017		2020		2023	
	Average ($1,000s)	Share of revenue (%)	Average ($1,000s)	Share of revenue (%)	Average ($1,000s)	Share of revenue (%)
Revenue	14,726	100.0	14,214	100.0	17,903	100.0
Cost of sales						
Land costs	2,547	17.3	2,523	17.8	2,003	11.2
Direct costs: single-family	8,103	55.0	8,378	58.9	10,908	60.9
Direct costs: multifamily, remodeling, light commercial/industrial	629	4.3	30	0.2	225	1.3
Indirect construction costs	363	2.5	537	3.8	657	3.7
Other costs	10	0.1	9	0.1	86	0.5
Total cost of sales	11,652	79.1	11,476	80.7	13,880	77.5
Gross profit	**3,074**	**20.9**	**2,738**	**19.3**	**4,023**	**22.5**

[4] Increased production of townhouses (which generally have lower land costs than detached units) helps explain the drop: in 2023, 17% of all single-family starts were attached — the highest on record for data going back to 1985.

Comparing the gross performance in 2023 of the three different types of business models analyzed in this study — *builders with land costs, builders without land costs,* and *combination builders,* those with land costs achieved the highest gross profit margin, at 22.5%. In contrast, the average gross margin was 18.7% among builders without land costs and 16.6% among combination builders (Appendix IV.1).

On a net basis, builders with land costs lost money in fiscal years 2008 (-4.9%) and 2010 (-1.0%), in large part due to running their businesses with operating expenses that exceeded 18% of total revenue. Years later, after reigning in and lowering these expenses to 10.6% in 2017, they achieved an until-then record 10.3% net profit margin. In 2020, however, operating expenses regained strength and their net margin fell to 6.6%. But in 2023, with a record high gross profit margin and slightly lower operating expenses accounting for 11.9% of revenue, builders with land costs averaged a 10.6% net profit margin ($1.9 million) — a new all-time high for the group (Table 2.2). Figure 2.1 summarizes the income statement for builders with land costs for 2023.

Table 2.2. Net profit

	2017		2020		2023	
	Average ($1,000s)	Share of revenue (%)	Average ($1,000s)	Share of revenue (%)	Average ($1,000s)	Share of revenue (%)
Gross profit	3,074	20.9	2,738	19.3	4,023	22.5
Operating expenses						
Financing expenses	233	1.6	253	1.8	408	2.3
Sales & mktg. expenses	670	4.5	744	5.2	701	3.9
General & administrative expenses	493	3.4	678	4.8	742	4.1
Depreciation	11	0.1	6	0.0	14	0.1
Owner's compensation	153	1.0	115	0.8	262	1.5
Total operating expenses	1,559	10.6	1,795	12.6	2,128	11.9
Net profit (loss)	**1,514**	**10.3**	**943**	**6.6**	**1,895**	**10.6**

Among the three business models analyzed in this study, builders with land costs had the highest net profit margin in 2023, at 10.6%, followed by combination builders, at 7.4%. The lowest average net margin in 2023 belonged to builders without land costs, at 3.0% (Appendix IV.1).

Figure 2.1. Cost of sales, expenses, and net profit (% of revenue)

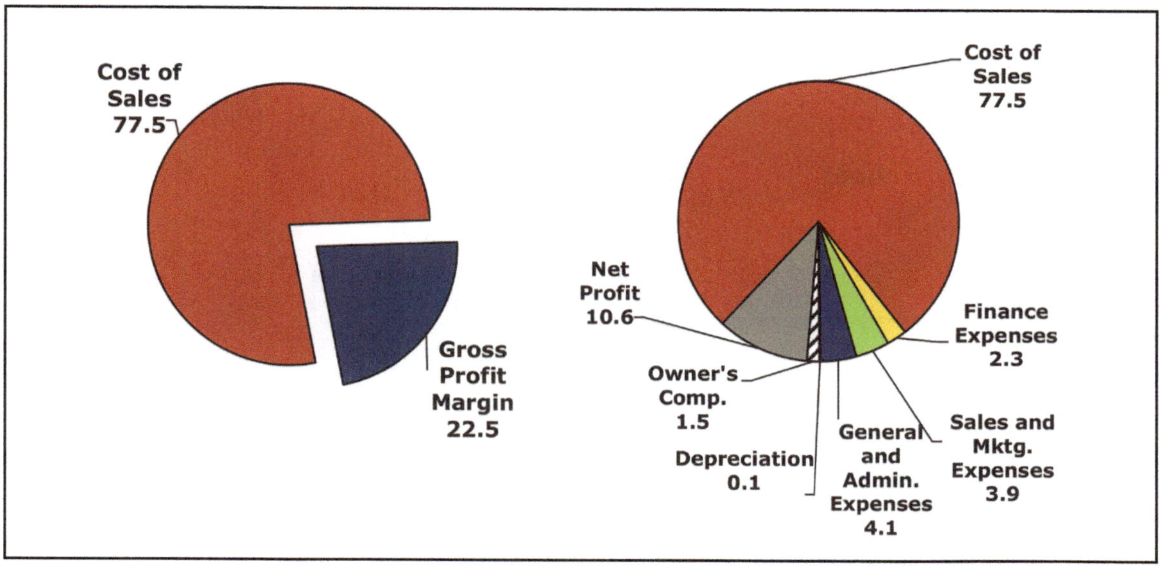

The balance sheet for the average builder with land costs was larger in 2023 ($10.9 million in assets) than in 2020 ($9.5 million) and 2017 ($8.6 million). Most of the assets (58.0%) were held as construction work in progress and 11.1% was held in cash — the second study in a row this share has exceeded 10% for builders with land costs. Other non-current assets (e.g., refundable deposits and furnished model homes) represented 16.5% of assets in 2023, which means current assets made up the remaining 83.5% — down from 91.3% in 2020 and more in line with the 84.4% share in 2017 (Table 2.3).

On the liabilities side of the ledger, builders with land costs shifted their debt positions away from current liabilities toward long-term debt. More specifically, from 2020 to 2023, their total current liabilities went from financing 56.3% of assets ($5.3 million) to 38.5% ($4.2 million), while long-term debt jumped from 12.6% ($1.2 million) to 21.5% ($2.3 million). Altogether, builders with land costs financed 60.0% of their assets through debt in 2023, down from 69.0% in 2020 and 64.4% in 2017.

Lower levels of debt meant builders with land costs relied more heavily on their own invested capital to finance their operations. Owner's equity in 2023 supported 40.0% of their assets, the highest equity share in the history of the series for this group of builders.

Table 2.3. Balance sheet

	2017		2020		2023	
	Average ($1,000s)	Share of total (%)	Average ($1,000s)	Share of total (%)	Average ($1,000s)	Share of total (%)
Assets						
Current assets						
Cash	686	8.0	1,189	12.6	1,209	11.1
Receivables & Inventories	674	7.8	451	4.8	806	7.4
Construction work in progress	5,282	61.2	6,546	69.2	6,320	58.0
Other current assets	636	7.4	453	4.8	764	7.0
Total current assets	7,278	84.4	8,640	91.3	9,099	83.5
Other assets	1,350	15.6	823	8.7	1,804	16.5
Total assets	**8,628**	**100.0**	**9,463**	**100.0**	**10,903**	**100.0**
Liabilities						
Current liabilities	1,042	12.1	2,985	31.5	787	7.2
Construction loans payable	3,393	39.3	2,344	24.8	3,410	31.3
Total current liabilities	4,434	51.4	5,329	56.3	4,197	38.5
Long-term loans payable	1,010	11.7	1,117	11.8	910	8.4
Other long-term liabilities	108	1.3	80	0.8	1,430	13.1
Total liabilities	**5,553**	**64.4**	**6,525**	**69.0**	**6,537**	**60.0**
Owner's equity	**3,075**	**35.6**	**2,938**	**31.0**	**4,366**	**40.0**
Total liabilities & owner's equity	**8,628**	**100.0**	**9,463**	**100.0**	**10,903**	**100.0**

All financial ratios point to a solid improvement in the performance of builders with land costs from 2020 to 2023. To start, the steep decline in short-term debt caused the current ratio to surge from 1.62 to 2.17, which means they went from having 62% more current assets than current liabilities to 117% during this period. In addition, the record levels of capital investment described earlier led the debt-to-equity ratio to fall from 2.22 to 1.50, evidencing lower levels of risk. Finally, record net profit margins produced significant improvements in this group's ROA (10.0% to 17.4%) and ROE (32.1% to 43.4%) between 2020 and 2023 (Table 2.4).

Table 2.4. Financial ratios

	2017	2020	2023
Current ratio	1.64	1.62	2.17
Debt-to-equity ratio	1.81	2.22	1.50
Return on assets (%)	17.6	10.0	17.4
Return on equity (%)	49.2	32.1	43.4

Note: No data for the top and bottom 25% of builders with land costs were produced because of insufficient sample size.

3

Builders Without Land Costs

Builders without land costs (those that build exclusively on their customers' land) responding to the survey in 2023 were smaller companies than in 2020. This group of respondents brought in an average of $4.7 million in revenue in 2023, down 46% from the series record of $8.7 million in 2020 and 23% less than in 2017 ($6.1 million) (Table 3.1). The substantial reduction in total revenue stemmed from running smaller operations across all market segments: single-family home building, residential remodeling, multifamily, and light commercial.

All costs of sales combined accounted for an average 81.3% of this group's revenue in 2023, down from 86.8% in 2020. Not surprisingly, given the drop in revenue from remodeling, multifamily, and light commercial, much of the decline came from lower direct construction costs for these activities, which dropped from 24.1% of revenue to just 9.7%. That left builders without land costs with an average gross profit margin of 18.7% in 2023 ($877,000), ahead of both 2020 (13.2%) and 2017 (15.3%).

Table 3.1. Gross profit

	2017		2020		2023	
	Average ($1,000s)	**Share of revenue (%)**	**Average ($1,000s)**	**Share of revenue (%)**	**Average ($1,000s)**	**Share of revenue (%)**
Revenue	6,076	100.0	8,692	100.0	4,685	100.0
Cost of sales						
Land costs	0	0.0	0	0.0	0	0.0
Direct costs: single-family	4,787	78.8	5,414	62.3	3,270	69.8
Direct costs: multifamily, remodeling, light commercial/industrial	184	3.0	2,091	24.1	455	9.7
Indirect construction costs	103	1.7	43	0.5	68	1.5
Other costs	72	1.2	0	0.0	14	0.3
Total cost of sales	5,145	84.7	7,548	86.8	3,808	81.3
Gross profit	**931**	**15.3**	**1,143**	**13.2**	**877**	**18.7**

In contrast to the considerable reduction in costs of sales, the share of revenue builders without land costs spent on operating expenses rose by more than seven percentage points from 2020 to 2023, jumping from 8.6% to 15.8% (Table 3.2). All expense lines increased vis-a-vis revenue, but growth was most pronounced in the general and administrative categories (e.g., salaries, vehicles, insurance, etc.), which rose from 4.6% to 9.1%. In the end, this group of builders reported an average net profit margin of only 3.0% in 2023, down from 4.5% in 2020 and 4.3% in 2017. It was also the group's lowest net margin since 2010 (2.9%). Figure 3.1 summarizes the income statement for builders without land costs for 2023.

Table 3.2. Net profit

	2017		2020		2023	
	Average ($1,000s)	Share of revenue (%)	Average ($1,000s)	Share of revenue (%)	Average ($1,000s)	Share of revenue (%)
Gross profit	931	15.3	1,143	13.2	877	18.7
Operating expenses						
Financing expenses	7	0.1	3	0.0	3	0.1
Sales & mktg. expenses	38	0.6	27	0.3	94	2.0
General & administrative expenses	426	7.0	396	4.6	428	9.1
Depreciation	11	0.2	22	0.2	16	0.3
Owner's compensation	191	3.1	301	3.5	198	4.2
Total operating expenses	673	11.1	748	8.6	738	15.8
Net profit (loss)	**258**	**4.3**	**395**	**4.5**	**139**	**3.0**

Figure 3.1 Cost of sales, expenses, and net profit (% of revenue)

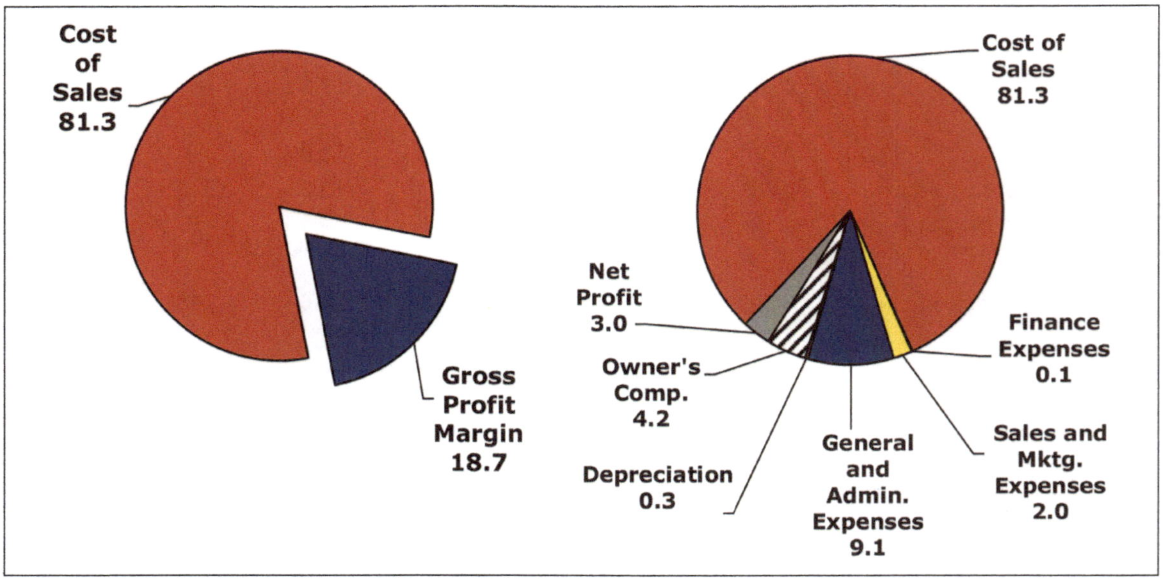

On average, total assets among builders without land costs responding to the survey averaged $2.2 million in 2023, 60% lower than an anomalously high $5.4 million in 2020. The bulk of the drop came from the amount held as construction work in progress, which fell from 80.7% of assets ($4.3 million) to 46.7% ($1.0 million). The vast majority of the group's assets (91.9%) were current assets, including 26.5% in cash (Table 3.3).

These builders also dramatically changed how they financed their companies in 2023. That year, they held an average $1.7 million in total liabilities, which means 76.2% of their assets were backed up by debt. In 2020, the share was only 27.8%. Such increased reliance on all forms of debt (both short- and long-term) indicates builders without land costs used much less of their own capital to finance their companies, which is shown by the drop in the equity share from 72.2% ($3.9 million) in 2020 to 23.8% ($519,000) in 2023.

Table 3.3. Balance sheet

	2017		2020		2023	
	Average ($1,000s)	Share of total (%)	Average ($1,000s)	Share of total (%)	Average ($1,000s)	Share of total (%)
Assets						
Current assets						
Cash	307	22.7	294	5.5	578	26.5
Receivables and Inventories	441	32.6	464	8.6	234	10.7
Construction work in progress	432	31.9	4,344	80.7	1,018	46.7
Other current assets	48	3.6	133	2.5	173	7.9
Total current assets	1,229	90.8	5,235	97.3	2,002	91.9
Other assets	125	9.2	148	2.7	177	8.1
Total assets	**1,353**	**100.0**	**5,383**	**100.0**	**2,180**	**100.0**
Liabilities						
Current liabilities	559	41.3	1,433	26.6	1,029	47.2
Construction loans payable	71	5.3	4	0.1	29	1.3
Total current liabilities	630	46.5	1,437	26.7	1,058	48.5
Long-term loans payable	23	1.7	58	1.1	89	4.1
Other long-term liabilities	15	1.1	3	0.1	514	23.6
Total liabilities	**668**	**49.4**	**1,499**	**27.8**	**1,661**	**76.2**
Owner's equity	**685**	**50.6**	**3,884**	**72.2**	**519**	**23.8**
Total liabilities & owner's equity	**1,353**	**100.0**	**5,383**	**100.0**	**2,180**	**100.0**

The current ratio for this group of builders was 1.89 in 2023, down significantly from 2020 (3.64) and more in line with where it stood in 2017 (1.95) (Table 3.4). As a reminder, the current ratio is a liquidity measure that evaluates a company's ability to repay its short-term liabilities using its short-term assets. In general, the higher the current ratio is, the better the company's financial health.

With a balance sheet showing a shift from equity to debt financing, it is not surprising to see the debt-to-equity ratio — a measure of leverage and risk — jumping from 0.39 in 2020 to 3.20 in 2023. That means builders without land costs had 3.2 times more debt than equity! Meanwhile, pushed down by lower returns and lower assets, ROA continued to fall for this group of builders, going from 7.3% in 2020 to 6.4% in 2023. Their ROE did strengthen, from 10.2% to 26.8%, but only because the drop in equity was proportionately higher than in returns

Table 3.4. Financial ratios

	2017	2020	2023
Current ratio	1.95	3.64	1.89
Debt-to-equity ratio	0.97	0.39	3.20
Return on assets (%)	19.1	7.3	6.4
Return on equity (%)	37.7	10.2	26.8

Note: No data for the top and bottom 25% of builders without land costs were produced because of insufficient sample size.

4

Combination Builders

In this study, combination builders are defined as those who build homes on their land and on land owned by their customers. This hybrid group of builders averaged $11.5 million in total revenue during 2023, 25% lower than in 2020 ($15.2 million) and 42% lower than in 2017 ($19.9 million) (Table 4.1). Comparing cost structures from 2020 to 2023 shows the share of revenue spent on direct construction costs to build single-family homes rose from 63.8% to 69.3%, while the share spent on land costs fell from 10.5% to 6.2%. In other words, labor, subcontractors, and materials consumed a larger slice of revenue while land costs took a smaller share. Added together, all items under costs of sales represented 83.4% of the total revenue combination builders generated in 2023 (up slightly from 82.3% in 2020), leaving them with an average gross profit margin of 16.6% ($1.9 million), which is marginally lower than in 2020 (17.7%) and 2017 (17.2%).

Table 4.1. Gross profit

	2017		2020		2023	
	Average ($1,000s)	**Share of revenue (%)**	**Average ($1,000s)**	**Share of revenue (%)**	**Average ($1,000s)**	**Share of revenue (%)**
Revenue	19,917	100.0	15,211	100.0	11,466	100.0
Cost of sales						
Land costs	2,060	10.3	1,603	10.5	711	6.2
Direct costs: single-family	13,344	67.0	9,707	63.8	7,945	69.3
Direct costs: multifamily, remodeling, light commercial/industrial	380	1.9	804	5.3	614	5.4
Indirect construction costs	641	3.2	399	2.6	237	2.1
Other costs	59	0.3	5	0.0	58	0.5
Total cost of sales	16,483	82.8	12,519	82.3	9,566	83.4
Gross profit	**3,434**	**17.2**	**2,692**	**17.7**	**1,900**	**16.6**

Combination builders spent a lower share of their revenue on operating expenses in 2023 (9.1%) than in 2020 (10.5%). The most important reduction happened around sales and marketing expenses, which went from taking up 3.8% of revenue to just 1.3%. Financing expenses also declined, but to a lesser extent (1.2% to 0.5%). The only expense line combination builders were unable to shrink was general and administrative expenses, which rose from 3.9% of revenue to 6.1%. As shown in other chapters, this increase in G&A expenses from 2020 to 2023 was widespread across different types of builders, likely linked to increased salaries and benefits for non-job-related personnel.

After subtracting all expenses, combination builders posted an average net profit margin of 7.4% ($854,000), ahead of both 2020 (7.2%) and 2017 (5.3%), and the second highest in the history of the series after 2014's 7.6% (Table 4.2). Figure 4.1 summarizes the income statement for combination builders for 2023.

Table 4.2. Net profit

	2017		2020		2023	
	Average ($1,000s)	Share of revenue (%)	Average ($1,000s)	Share of revenue (%)	Average ($1,000s)	Share of revenue (%)
Gross profit	3,434	17.2	2,692	17.7	1,900	16.6
Operating expenses						
Financing expenses	228	1.1	186	1.2	52	0.5
Sales & mktg. expenses	1,027	5.2	576	3.8	147	1.3
General & administrative expenses	901	4.5	589	3.9	705	6.1
Depreciation	28	0.1	33	0.2	12	0.1
Owner's compensation	186	0.9	206	1.4	130	1.1
Total operating expenses	2,370	11.9	1,590	10.5	1,046	9.1
Net profit (loss)	**1,064**	**5.3**	**1,102**	**7.2**	**854**	**7.4**

Figure 4.1. Cost of sales, expenses, and net profit (% of revenue)

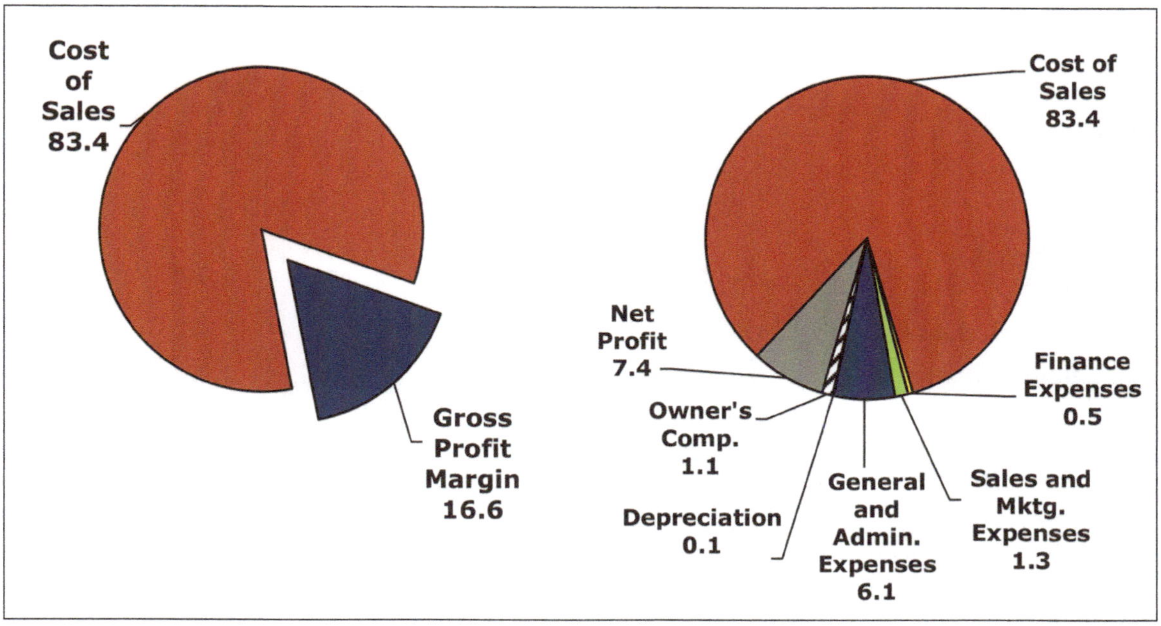

The average 2023 balance sheet among combination builders showed assets totaling \$6.9 million, about 26% lower than in 2020 (\$9.3 million) and 19% lower than in 2017 (\$8.5 million). The reduction in assets was accompanied by a change in their composition. Construction work in progress, for example, increased its share from 57.4% in 2020 to 67.3% in 2023. Receivables and inventories, meanwhile, declined from 12.4% to 5.7%. Combined, this group's current assets accounted for 95.6%, up from 90.7% in 2020 (Table 4.3).

Combination builders in 2023 continued financing their operations through a similar blend of debt and equity as they did in 2020. For example, current liabilities supported 53.4% of their assets in 2023, essentially unchanged from the 53.7% share in 2020. Total debt (current plus long-term) financed 62.7% of this group's assets, not far from the 62.8% in 2020. Put differently, combination builders maintained their capital investment about constant between 2020 and 2023, financing 37.3% and 37.2% of their assets through equity, respectively.

Table 4.3. Balance sheet

	2017		2020		2023	
	Average ($1,000s)	Share of total (%)	Average ($1,000s)	Share of total (%)	Average ($1,000s)	Share of total (%)
Assets						
Current assets						
Cash	469	5.5	1,307	14.0	1,132	16.3
Receivables and inventories	583	6.8	1,158	12.4	397	5.7
Construction work in progress	6,279	73.6	5,355	57.4	4,666	67.3
Other current assets	589	6.9	630	6.8	427	6.2
Total current assets	7,920	92.9	8,450	90.7	6,622	95.6
Other assets	608	7.1	871	9.3	306	4.4
Total assets	**8,528**	**100.0**	**9,321**	**100.0**	**6,928**	**100.0**
Liabilities						
Current liabilities	3,050	35.8	2,656	28.5	1,715	24.8
Construction loans payable	2,414	28.3	2,352	25.2	1,985	28.7
Total current liabilities	5,464	64.1	5,008	53.7	3,700	53.4
Long-term loans payable	526	6.2	634	6.8	453	6.5
Other long-term liabilities	40	0.5	209	2.2	189	2.7
Total liabilities	**6,031**	**70.7**	**5,851**	**62.8**	**4,342**	**62.7**
Owner's equity	**2,497**	**29.3**	**3,470**	**37.2**	**2,586**	**37.3**
Total liabilities & owner's equity	**8,528**	**100.0**	**9,321**	**100.0**	**6,928**	**100.0**

Changes of similar proportions in returns, assets, and equity from 2020 to 2023 meant little change in financial ratios for combination builders during this period (Table 4.4). The debt-to-equity ratio remained about the same, going from 1.69 to 1.68, continuing to indicate low and stable levels of risk. The current ratio revealed comparable levels of liquidity, barely edging up from 1.69 to 1.79 during this period. ROA and ROE, meanwhile, showed steadiness in the group's ability to convert assets and equity into profits. In 2023, returns were equivalent to 12.3% of their assets and 33.0% of their equity, not significantly different from 11.8% and 31.8%, respectively, in 2020.

Table 4.4. Financial ratios

	2017	2020	2023
Current ratio	1.45	1.69	1.79
Debt-to-equity ratio	2.42	1.69	1.68
Return on assets (%)	12.50	11.80	12.3
Return on equity (%)	42.60	31.80	33.0

Note: No data for the top and bottom 25% of combination builders were produced because of insufficient sample size.

5

Small-Volume Builders

All Small-Volume Builders Combined

A small-volume builder, as defined in this study, closes 25 or fewer units per year. According to the 2023 NAHB Builder Member Census, approximately 82% of our association's single-family builders fall under this classification. Total revenue for the typical small-volume builder in 2023 was $5.2 million, 4% lower than in 2020 ($5.4 million) but 19% higher than in 2017 ($4.4 million). On average, total costs of sales utilized 82.3% of revenue, a smaller share than in 2020 (86.4%). Most of the decline came from fewer direct construction costs for remodeling, multifamily, and light commercial building, which dropped from 12.9% to 5.7% (revenue from those activities also declined). That left small-volume builders with an average gross profit margin of 17.7% ($925,000) — an improvement over the gross margin in 2020 (13.6%) and 2017 (16.8%) (Table 5.1).

Table 5.1. Gross profit

	2017		2020		2023	
	Average ($1,000s)	**Share of revenue (%)**	**Average ($1,000s)**	**Share of revenue (%)**	**Average ($1,000s)**	**Share of revenue (%)**
Revenue	4,400	100.0	5,432	100.0	5,236	100.0
Cost of Sales						
Land costs	347	7.9	335	6.2	216	4.1
Direct costs: single-family	2,973	67.6	3,546	65.3	3,647	69.7
Direct costs: multifamily, remodeling, light commercial/industrial	217	4.9	702	12.9	296	5.7
Indirect construction costs	119	2.7	106	1.9	112	2.1
Other costs	6	0.1	4	0.1	41	0.8
Total cost of Sales	3,662	83.2	4,693	86.4	4,312	82.3
Gross profit	**737**	**16.8**	**740**	**13.6**	**925**	**17.7**

Small-volume builders spent an average of $705,000 on operating expenses in 2023. More than half of that amount paid for general and administrative expenses ($403,000), which took up a significantly higher share of revenue (7.7%) than in 2020 (4.5%). Due to higher G&A expenses, and despite keeping a lid on all other expense lines, overall operating expenses for this group of builders averaged 13.5% of revenue in 2023, ahead of 2020's 9.8%. In the end, gains in gross margins saved small-volume builders from increased expenses and allowed them to post an average net profit margin of 4.2% in 2023, slightly ahead of the 3.8% reported in 2020 (but lower than 2017's 5.7%) (Table 5.2). Figure 5.1 summarizes the income statement for small-volume builders for 2023 (Appendix IV.3).

Table 5.2. Net profit

	2017		2020		2023	
	Average ($1,000s)	Share of revenue (%)	Average ($1,000s)	Share of revenue (%)	Average ($1,000s)	Share of revenue (%)
Gross profit	737	16.8	740	13.6	925	17.7
Operating expenses						
Financing expenses	30	0.7	39	0.7	37	0.7
Sales & mktg. expenses	104	2.4	73	1.3	92	1.8
General & administrative expenses	229	5.2	244	4.5	403	7.7
Depreciation	5	0.1	12	0.2	14	0.3
Owner's compensation	118	2.7	165	3.0	159	3.0
Total operating expenses	486	11.0	533	9.8	705	13.5
Net profit (loss)	**251**	**5.7**	**207**	**3.8**	**220**	**4.2**

Figure 5.1. Cost of sales, expenses, and net profit (% of revenue)

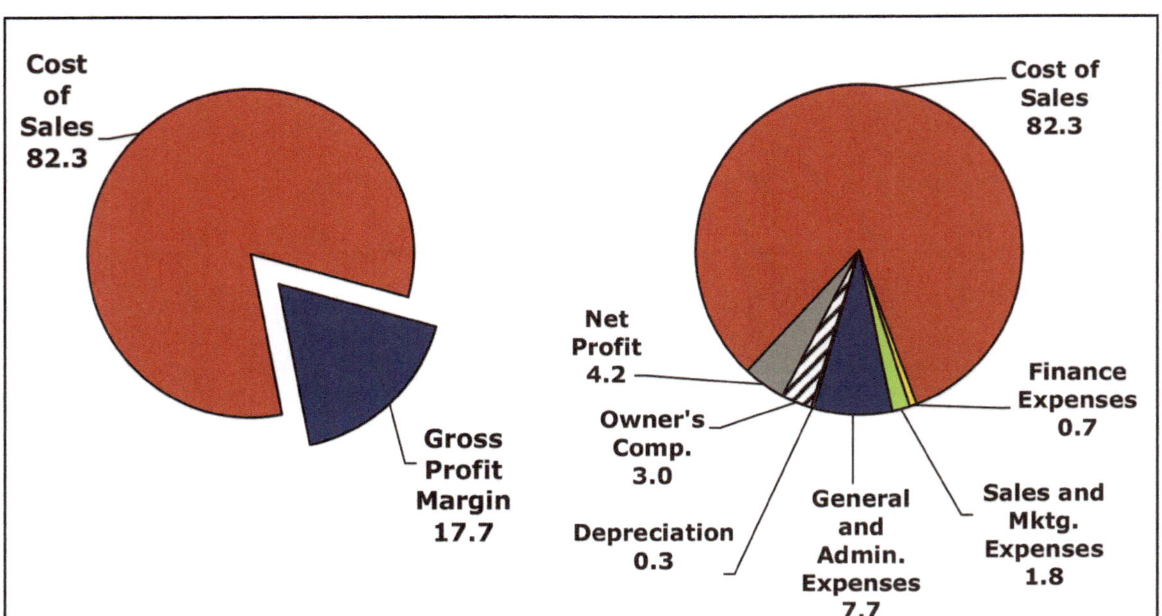

Small-volume builders reported average total assets of $2.8 million in 2023, of which 48.7% was tied to construction work in progress and 21.0% to cash (Table 5.3). The level of assets in 2023 was 22% lower than in 2020 ($3.6 million) but 58% ahead of 2017 ($1.8 million). The vast majority of this group's assets (91.7%) were current (i.e., easily convertible to cash within the next operating cycle, usually one year), which means that only a small fraction (8.3%) was fixed (i.e., long-term tangible property).

The other side of the ledger shows that small builders continued to increase their reliance on debt financing. In 2023, 74.0% of this group's assets were backed up by either short- or long-term liabilities, up from 42.9% in 2017 and 53.5% in 2020. The latter means small builders have reduced their investments and/or taken out more of their business profits, to the point where in 2023 only 26.0% of their assets were supported by equity, compared to 57.1% in 2017 and 46.5% in 2020.

Table 5.3. Balance sheet

	2017		2020		2023	
	Average ($1,000s)	**Share of total (%)**	**Average ($1,000s)**	**Share of total (%)**	**Average ($1,000s)**	**Share of total (%)**
Assets						
Current assets						
Cash	218	12.2	351	9.7	596	21.0
Receivables and Inventories	358	20.0	309	8.5	363	12.8
Construction work in Progress	613	34.2	2,583	71.1	1,382	48.7
Other current assets	107	6.0	278	7.6	259	9.1
Total current assets	1,296	72.3	3,521	96.9	2,599	91.7
Other assets	497	27.7	112	3.1	236	8.3
Total assets	**1,794**	**100.0**	**3,633**	**100.0**	**2,836**	**100.0**
Liabilities						
Current liabilities	392	21.8	951	26.2	1,038	36.6
Construction loans Payable	224	12.5	863	23.7	547	19.3
Total current liabilities	615	34.3	1,814	49.9	1,585	55.9
Long-term loans payable	84	4.7	95	2.6	131	4.6
Other long-term liabilities	71	3.9	33	0.9	383	13.5
Total liabilities	**770**	**42.9**	**1,942**	**53.5**	**2,100**	**74.0**
Owner's equity	**1,024**	**57.1**	**1,691**	**46.5**	**736**	**26.0**
Total liabilities & owner's equity	**1,794**	**100.0**	**3,633**	**100.0**	**2,836**	**100.0**

A disproportionate fall in current assets vis-a-vis current liabilities, along with higher levels of total debt, caused some deterioration in the financial health of the typical small-volume builder. The current ratio, for example, dropped to 1.64 from 1.94 in 2020, which means small builders are somewhat less able to cover their immediate debts with the amount of liquid assets they hold. Not surprisingly, the debt-to-equity ratio jumped to 2.85 from 1.15 in 2020, a clear illustration of small builders' heightened reliance on debt to run their businesses.

On the other hand, higher returns accompanied by a sharp drop in capital investments led to improvements in both their ROA and ROE. Return on assets rose to 7.7%, from 5.7% in 2020, while return on equity more than doubled, going from 12.2% in 2020 to 29.8% in 2023 (Table 5.4).

Table 5.4. Financial ratios

	2017	2020	2023
Current ratio	2.11	1.94	1.64
Debt-to-equity ratio	0.75	1.15	2.85
Return on assets (%)	14.00	5.70	7.70
Return on equity (%)	24.50	12.20	29.80

Small-Volume Builders with Land Costs

To provide builders reading this study the ability to compare their financial performance against their closest peers, the rest of this chapter breaks down small-volume builders into three different subsets: those with land costs, those without land costs, and combination builders. The analysis is presented only for subsets with enough responses to provide reliable results. This first section analyzes the performance of small-volume builders with land costs, in other words, builders with 25 or fewer closings a year who only build spec or pre-sold homes on their own lots.

Small-volume builders with land costs responding in 2023 were significantly smaller companies than similar builders responding to previous iterations of this study. That conclusion is derived from analyzing their balance sheets, which show average total assets shrinking by 34%, from $2.6 million in 2020 to $1.7 million in 2023. The composition of those assets has also changed: whereas 98.1% of assets in 2020 were highly liquid–i.e., current–, that share dropped to 82.8% in 2023. And while construction work in progress dropped from accounting for 64.5% of assets to 43.5%, the share jumped for receivables and inventories from 5.1% to 25.6% (Table 5.5)

On average, small builders with land costs carried $1.1 million in total liabilities in 2023, which financed 64.2% of their assets. That shows somewhat less reliance on debt than in 2020 when the share was 70.0%. The latter implies a modest increase in the relevance of invested capital, as the owners' equity share in their businesses rose from 30.0% in 2020 to 35.8% in 2023.

Table 5.5. Small-volume builders with land costs: balance sheet

	2017		2020		2023	
	Average ($1,000s)	**Share of total (%)**	**Average ($1,000s)**	**Share of total (%)**	**Average ($1,000s)**	**Share of total (%)**
Assets						
Current assets						
Cash	N/A		305	11.8	89	5.2
Receivables and inventories			134	5.1	438	25.6
Construction work in progress			1,676	64.5	745	43.5
Other current assets			433	16.7	148	8.6
Total current assets			2,547	98.1	1,420	82.8
Other assets			49	1.9	294	17.2
Total assets			**2,597**	**100.0**	**1,714**	**100.0**
Liabilities						
Current liabilities			383	14.7	195	11.4
Construction loans payable			1,250	48.2	718	41.9
Total current liabilities			1,633	62.9	913	53.2
Long-term loans payable			152	5.8	143	8.3
Other long-term liabilities			32	1.2	45	2.6
Total liabilities			**1,817**	**70.0**	**1,100**	**64.2**
Owner's equity			**780**	**30.0**	**614**	**35.8**
Total liabilities & owner's equity			**2,597**	**100.0**	**1,714**	**100.0**

With no income statement data available for small builders with land costs due to insufficient responses, important measures of profitability (ROA and ROE) cannot be calculated for this group of builders in 2023. The two financial ratios that can be constructed from the group's average balance sheet, however, point to improving financial health for these builders. The current ratio, for example, saw a slight increase, from 1.48 in 2020 to 1.56 in 2023, while the debt-to-equity ratio dropped from 2.29 to 1.79 (Table 5.6)

Table 5.6. Small-volume builders with land costs: financial ratios

	2017	2020	2023
Current ratio	N/A	1.48	1.56
Debt-to-equity ratio		2.29	1.79
Return on assets (%)		1.30	N/A
Return on equity (%)		4.40	N/A

Small-Volume Builders without Land Costs

Small-volume builders without land costs (25 or fewer closings who only build on land owned by their customers) reported average revenue of $5.2 million in 2023, about 40% lower than in 2020 ($8.7 million) (Table 5.7). Not surprisingly, given falling revenue from remodeling, multifamily, and light commercial building during this period, they spent far less on direct construction costs for these activities in 2023 (9.9% of revenue) than in 2020 (24.1%). Altogether, their cost of sales accounted for 82.1% of revenue, somewhat lower than in 2020 (86.8%). As a result, small builders without land costs posted an average gross profit margin of 17.9%, significantly higher than in 2020 (13.2%) and the highest gross margin for this group since 2008 (19.9%).

Table 5.7. Small-volume builders without land costs: gross profit

	2017		2020		2023	
	Average ($1,000s)	Share of revenue (%)	Average ($1,000s)	Share of revenue (%)	Average ($1,000s)	Share of revenue (%)
Revenue	N/A		8,692	100.0	5,222	100.0
Cost of sales						
Land costs			0	0.0	0	0.0
Direct costs: single-family			5,414	62.3	3,684	70.5
Direct costs: multifamily, remodeling, light commercial/industrial			2,091	24.1	515	9.9
Indirect construction costs			43	0.5	72	1.4
Other costs			0	0.0	18	0.4
Total cost of sales			7,548	86.8	4,289	82.1
Gross profit			**1,143**	**13.2**	**933**	**17.9**

Meanwhile, driven by a near doubling of general and administrative expenses (from 4.6% of revenue in 2020 to 8.8% in 2023), total operating expenses for small-volume builders without land costs exploded from 8.6% to 15.9% during this period (Table 5.8). As a result, this group averaged a mere 1.9% net profit margin ($102,000) in 2023, down from 4.5% in 2020 and the lowest in the history of the series for this cohort of builders. Figure 5.2 summarizes the income statement for small-volume builders without land costs for 2023 (Appendix IV.5).

Table 5.8. Small-volume builders without land costs: net profit

	2017		2020		2023	
	Average ($1,000s)	Share of revenue (%)	Average ($1,000s)	Share of revenue (%)	Average ($1,000s)	Share of revenue (%)
Gross profit	N/A		1,143	13.2	933	17.9
Operating expenses						
Financing expenses			3	0.0	2	0.0
Sales & mktg. expenses			27	0.3	116	2.2
General & administrative expenses			396	4.6	457	8.8
Depreciation			22	0.2	21	0.4
Owner's compensation			301	3.5	236	4.5
Total operating expenses			748	8.6	831	15.9
Net profit (loss)			**395**	**4.5**	**102**	**1.9**

Figure 5.2. Small-volume builders without land costs: cost of sales, expenses, and net profit (% of revenue)

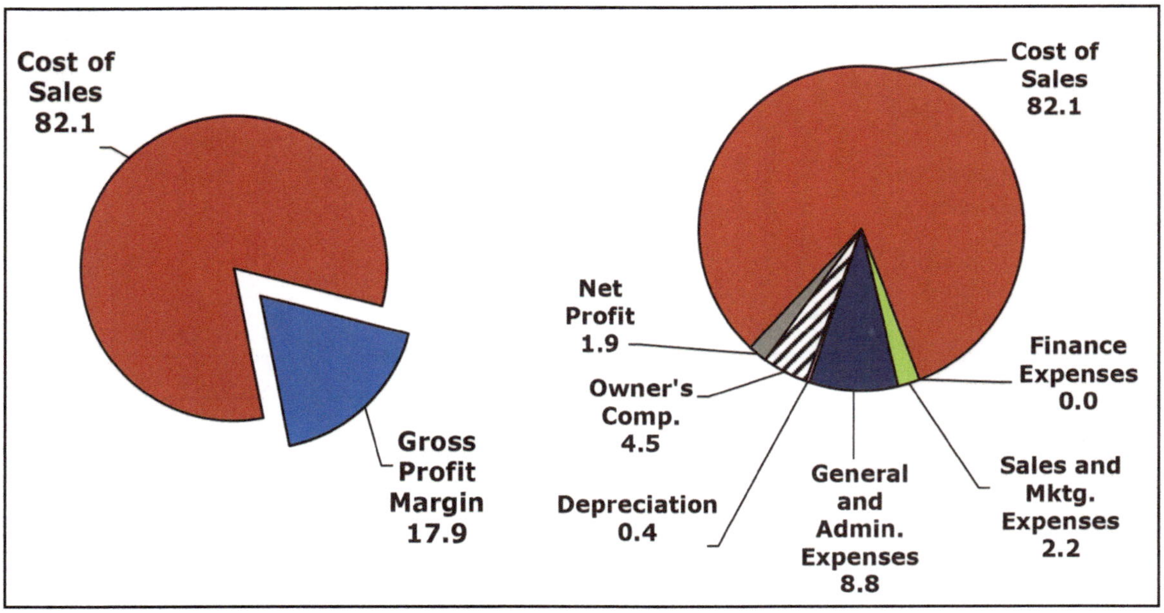

Small-volume builders without land costs had an average of $2.7 million in assets on their 2023 balance sheets, down 51% from a seemingly anomalous $5.4 million in 2020. Most of their assets (50.6%) were held as construction work in progress, followed by cash (25.8%). In all, current assets comprised 94.3% of all the group's assets, not significantly different from where that share stood in 2020 (97.3%) (Table 5.9). Meanwhile, short- and long-term liabilities were the financial support behind 78.3% of their assets in 2023, up from only 27.8% in 2020. The latter means that the capital these builders have invested in their companies represented a mere 21.7% of the assets on their 2023 balance sheets.

Table 5.9. Small-volume builders without land costs: balance sheet

	2017		2020		2023	
	Average ($1,000s)	Share of total (%)	Average ($1,000s)	Share of total (%)	Average ($1,000s)	Share of total (%)
Assets						
Current assets						
Cash			294	5.5	687	25.8
Receivables and Inventories			464	8.6	279	10.5
Construction work in Progress	N/A		4,344	80.7	1,346	50.6
Other current assets			133	2.5	198	7.4
Total current assets			5,235	97.3	2,511	94.3
Other assets			148	2.7	152	5.7
Total assets			**5,383**	**100.0**	**2,663**	**100.0**
Liabilities						
Current liabilities			1,433	26.6	1,309	49.1
Construction loans Payable			4	0.1	30	1.1
Total current liabilities			1,437	26.7	1,339	50.3
Long-term loans payable			58	1.1	62	2.3
Other long-term liabilities			3	0.1	685	25.7
Total liabilities			**1,499**	**27.8**	**2,085**	**78.3**
Owner's equity			**3,884**	**72.2**	**578**	**21.7**
Total liabilities & owner's equity			**5,383**	**100.0**	**2,663**	**100.0**

Higher debt levels and lower returns led to a deterioration in the financial health of small-volume builders without land costs in 2023. They saw a drastic loss in liquidity, as the current ratio fell to 1.88 from 3.64 in 2020. Their debt-to-equity ratio skyrocketed from 0.39 to 3.61, which means they went from having higher levels of equity than debt to owing three times the amount of capital invested in their businesses. Lower returns drove the group's ROA down from 7.3% in 2020 to 3.8% in 2023, while even larger losses in equity allowed the ROE to rise from 10.2% to 17.6% during this period (Table 5.10).

Table 5.10. Small-volume builders without land costs: financial ratios

	2017	2020	2023
Current ratio		3.64	1.88
Debt-to-equity ratio	N/A	0.39	3.61
Return on assets (%)		7.30	3.80
Return on equity (%)		10.20	17.60

Small-Volume Combination Builders

The final section of this chapter turns to the performance of combination small-volume builders, who are firms with 25 or fewer closings that build both on their land as well as on their customers' land. Unfortunately, not enough of this type of builder provided income statements to allow for the tabulation of average revenue and profit margins.

Total assets for small combination builders averaged $4.4 million in 2023, about 40% higher than in 2020 ($3.1 million). During this period, these builders became more likely to hold their assets in cash (14.6% in 2020 vs. 22.6% in 2023) and less likely to hold them as construction work in progress (61.5% vs. 49.0%). But like past studies, nearly all their assets (92.6% in 2023 vs. 95.3% in 2020) remained in the form of current assets — highly liquid assets that can easily be converted to cash.

Meanwhile, total liabilities for this group of builders averaged $3.2 million in 2023, which financed roughly 73.6% of all their assets — down slightly from 78.7% in 2020. Unlike other types of small builders, small combination builders increased capital investments in their own businesses from an average of $669,000 in 2020 to $1.2 million in 2023. As a result, the share of assets financed through equity increased from 21.3% to 26.4% during this period (Table 5.11) (Appendix IV.6).

Table 5.11. Small-volume combination builders: balance sheet

	2017		2020		2023	
	Average ($1,000s)	Share of total (%)	Average ($1,000s)	Share of total (%)	Average ($1,000s)	Share of total (%)
Assets						
Current assets						
Cash	264	23.6	458	14.6	988	22.6
Receivables and inventories	126	11.3	364	11.6	432	9.9
Construction work in progress	515	46.2	1,931	61.5	2,146	49.0
Other current assets	105	9.4	238	7.6	489	11.2
Total current assets	1,011	90.5	2,991	95.3	4,056	92.6
Other assets	106	9.5	148	4.7	324	7.4
Total assets	**1,116**	**100.0**	**3,139**	**100.0**	**4,380**	**100.0**
Liabilities						
Current liabilities	363	32.5	1,047	33.3	1,477	33.7
Construction loans payable	148	13.3	1,312	41.8	1,291	29.5
Total current liabilities	511	45.8	2,359	75.2	2,767	63.2
Long-term loans payable	22	2.0	49	1.5	244	5.6
Other long-term liabilities	7	0.6	63	2.0	214	4.9
Total liabilities	**540**	**48.4**	**2,470**	**78.7**	**3,225**	**73.6**
Owner's equity	**576**	**51.6**	**669**	**21.3**	**1,155**	**26.4**
Total liabilities & owner's equity	**1,116**	**100.0**	**3,139**	**100.0**	**4,380**	**100.0**

Relatively stronger growth in assets than in liabilities led to improvements in some financial ratios for small combination builders. The current ratio, for example, increased to 1.47, from 1.27 in 2020. The debt-to-equity ratio dropped to 2.79, after reaching a risky 3.69 in 2020 (Table 5.12). As a point of reference, a debt-to-equity ratio above 4.0 is considered so risky, that most financial institutions would likely turn down additional borrowing requests from any company with that level of debt. ROA and ROE cannot be calculated due to insufficient data to produce an average net profit margin for this group of builders.

Table 5.12. Small-volume combination builders: financial ratios

	2017	2020	2023
Current ratio	1.98	1.27	1.47
Debt-to-equity ratio	0.94	3.69	2.79
Return on assets (%)	N/A	8.00	N/A
Return on equity (%)	N/A	37.50	N/A

6

Production Builders

All Production Builders Combined

For this study, a production builder closes 26 or more units per year. According to the 2023 NAHB Builder Member Census, approximately 18% of our association's single-family builder members fall under this classification. Total revenue for the average production builder in 2023 was $20.3 million, around 30% less than in 2020 ($29.6 million) and 2017 ($29.8 million). On average, these builders spent 78.2% of revenue ($15.9 million) on costs of sales, down from 80.6% in 2020. Most of the cost reduction was from land costs, which as a share of revenue declined from 14.8% in 2020 to 10.0% in 2023. Production builders finished the 2023 fiscal year with an average gross profit margin of 21.8% ($4.4 million) — the largest gross profit margin for this group of builders in the history of the study (Table 6.1).

Table 6.1. Gross profit

	2017		2020		2023	
	Average ($1,000s)	**Share of revenue (%)**	**Average ($1,000s)**	**Share of revenue (%)**	**Average ($1,000s)**	**Share of revenue (%)**
Revenue	29,766	100.0	29,568	100.0	20,331	100.0
Cost of sales						
Land costs	3,870	13.0	4,388	14.8	2,025	10.0
Direct costs: single-family	18,613	62.5	17,751	60.0	12,586	61.9
Direct costs: multifamily, remodeling, light commercial/industrial	744	2.5	730	2.5	537	2.6
Indirect construction costs	836	2.8	950	3.2	673	3.3
Other costs	95	0.3	10	0.0	68	0.3
Total cost of sales	24,158	81.2	23,830	80.6	15,889	78.2
Gross profit	**5,608**	**18.8**	**5,738**	**19.4**	**4,441**	**21.8**

In addition to squeezing costs of sales to a record low, production builders also kept a tight belt around operating expense. In 2023, they spent 11.4% of revenue on expenses, essentially unchanged from 2020 (11.8%). In sharp contrast and as a reference, at their peak in 2008, production builders spent 18.9% of revenue on these expenses. They finished the 2023 fiscal year with an average \$2.1 million in net profits, which translates into a 10.4% net profit margin. This set a new record for this group, topping the previous highest net margin of 8.4% reported in 2006 (Table 6.2). Figure 6.1 summarizes the income statement for production builders in 2023 (Appendix IV.3).

Table 6.2. Net profit

	2017		2020		2023	
	Average (\$1,000s)	Share of revenue (%)	Average (\$1,000s)	Share of revenue (%)	Average (\$1,000s)	Share of revenue (%)
Gross profit	5,608	18.8	5,738	19.4	4,441	21.8
Operating expenses						
Financing expenses	398	1.3	457	1.5	381	1.9
Sales & mktg. expenses	1,479	5.0	1,473	5.0	730	3.6
General & administrative expenses	1,220	4.1	1,301	4.4	911	4.5
Depreciation	35	0.1	30	0.1	15	0.1
Owner's compensation	254	0.9	219	0.7	288	1.4
Total operating expenses	3,386	11.4	3,481	11.8	2,324	11.4
Net profit (loss)	**2,221**	**7.5**	**2,257**	**7.6**	**2,117**	**10.4**

Figure 6.1. Cost of sales, expenses, and net profit (% of revenue)

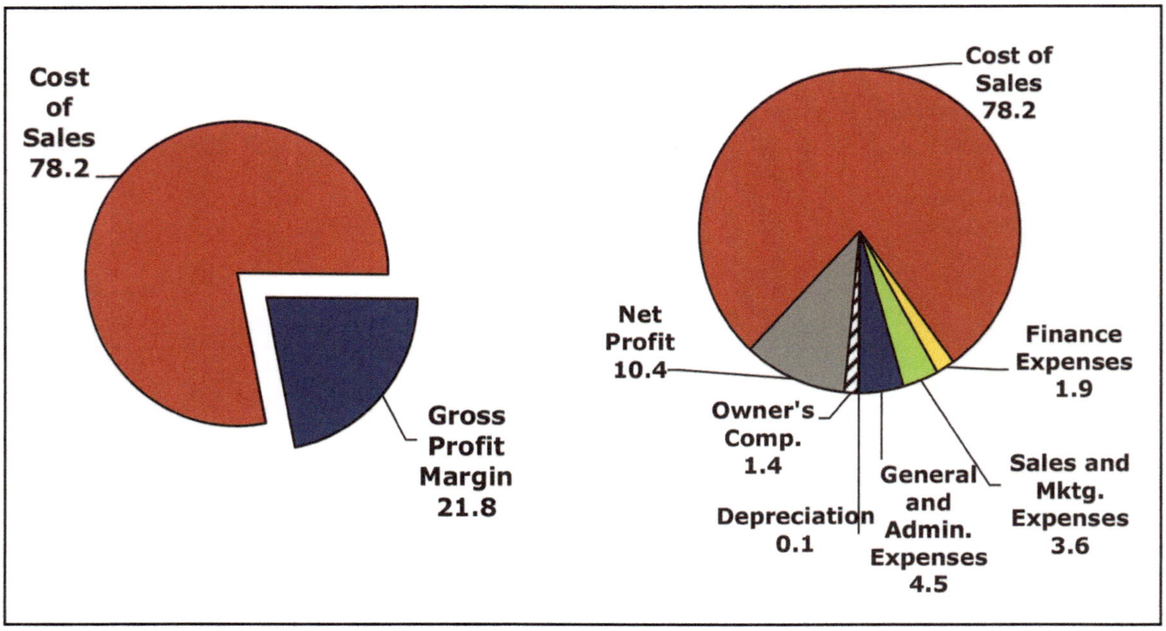

Production builders had smaller balance sheets in 2023 than in recent years, with total assets averaging $12.5 million, 26% lower than in 2020 ($16.9 million) and 13% lower than in 2017 ($14.5 million). There were no significant shifts in the composition of assets between 2020 and 2023, however, current assets accounted for 85.7% of all assets, only slightly lower than in 2020 (89.9%) (Table 6.3).

The recent decline in assets was accompanied by a substantial debt reduction. From 2020 to 2023, this group's total liabilities shrank by 32%, from $10.9 million to $7.4 million. The deleveraging dropped the share of their assets financed through debt from 64.2% in 2020 to 58.7% in 2023. Equity, meanwhile, only fell by 15% during this period, going from $6.1 million to $5.2 million. As a result, the share of assets financed through the owners' invested capital rose from 35.8% to 41.3%.

Table 6.3. Balance sheet

	2017		2020		2023	
	Average ($1,000s)	**Share of total (%)**	**Average ($1,000s)**	**Share of total (%)**	**Average ($1,000s)**	**Share of total (%)**
Assets						
Current assets						
Cash	924	6.4	2,250	13.3	1,482	11.8
Receivables and inventories	905	6.3	1,439	8.5	713	5.7
Construction work in progress	10,440	72.2	10,769	63.5	7,767	62.0
Other current assets	1,034	7.2	774	4.6	780	6.2
Total current assets	13,302	92.0	15,233	89.9	10,742	85.7
Other assets	1,151	8.0	1,713	10.1	1,790	14.3
Total assets	**14,454**	**100.0**	**16,946**	**100.0**	**12,533**	**100.0**
Liabilities						
Current liabilities	3,819	26.4	5,271	31.1	1,143	9.1
Construction loans payable	5,141	35.6	3,582	21.1	3,735	29.8
Total current liabilities	8,960	62.0	8,853	52.2	4,878	38.9
Long-term loans payable	1,305	9.0	1,777	10.5	1,047	8.4
Other long-term liabilities	43	0.3	255	1.5	1,437	11.5
Total liabilities	**10,308**	**71.3**	**10,885**	**64.2**	**7,362**	**58.7**
Owner's equity	**4,146**	**28.7**	**6,061**	**35.8**	**5,170**	**41.3**
Total liabilities & owner's equity	**14,454**	**100.0**	**16,946**	**100.0**	**12,533**	**100.0**

The ratios analyzed in this study show production builders are financially healthy companies. That trend continued in 2023, when their current ratio rose to 2.20 from 1.72 in 2020, demonstrating further liquidity in their operations. Sharply lower debt levels drove the group's debt-to-equity ratio down to 1.42 from 1.80 in 2020, showcasing decreased tolerance for risk. Achieving higher returns with fewer assets and equity caused both the ROA and ROE to gain ground: returns on assets grew from 13.3% in 2020 to 16.9% in 2023, while returns on equity went from 37.2% to 40.9%, respectively (Table 6.4).

Table 6.4. Financial ratios

	2017	2020	2023
Current ratio	1.48	1.72	2.20
Debt-to-equity ratio	2.49	1.80	1.42
Return on assets (%)	15.40	13.30	16.90
Return on equity (%)	53.60	37.20	40.90

Production Builders with Land Costs

Analyzing the performance of production builders who have land costs (those building 26 or more homes per year on their lots as spec or pre-sold homes) reveals their profitability improved significantly in 2023. Despite experiencing a 12% drop in average total revenue, from $31.2 million in 2020 to $27.5 million in 2023, they managed to post a gross profit margin of 22.8% in 2023 ($6.3 million) — the highest ever reported by this group of builders. That impressive margin was achieved through a steep reduction in the share of revenue spent on land costs, which fell from 17.4% in 2020 to 11.1% in 2023. Overall, the average total cost of sales for production builders with land costs declined from 79.4% to 77.2% during this period (Table 6.5).

Table 6.5. Production builders with land costs: gross profit

	2017		2020		2023	
	Average ($1,000s)	Share of revenue (%)	Average ($1,000s)	Share of revenue (%)	Average ($1,000s)	Share of revenue (%)
Revenue			31,209	100.0	27,492	100.0
Cost of sales						
Land costs			5,418	17.4	3,054	11.1
Direct costs: single-family	N/A		18,186	58.3	16,677	60.7
Direct costs: multifamily, remodeling, light commercial/industrial			0	0	370	1.3
Indirect construction costs			1,167	3.7	1,012	3.7
Other costs			10	0.0	110	0.4
Total cost of sales			24,781	79.4	21,224	77.2
Gross profit			**6,428**	**20.6**	**6,268**	**22.8**

Further analysis of their income statements shows that production builders with land costs found a way to squeeze more fat out of their operating expenses. In 2020, they spent 13.1% of revenue on these expenses; by 2023, they cut that share down to 11.9% (Table 6.6). The expense line with the largest setback during this period was sales and marketing expenses, which declined from 5.7% of revenue to 4.1%.

After subtracting all expenses from gross profit, this group of builders posted an average net profit margin of 10.9% ($3.0 million), exceeding the previous high point of 9.3% in 2006. Figure 6.2 summarizes the 2023 income statement for production builders with land costs (Appendix IV.4).

Table 6.6. Production builders with land costs: net profit

	2017		2020		2023	
	Average ($1,000s)	Share of revenue (%)	Average ($1,000s)	Share of revenue (%)	Average ($1,000s)	Share of revenue (%)
Gross profit			6,428	20.6	6,268	22.8
Operating expenses						
Financing expenses	N/A		541	1.7	624	2.3
Sales & mktg. expenses			1,771	5.7	1,114	4.1
General & administrative expenses			1,600	5.1	1,122	4.1
Depreciation			10	0.0	15	0.1
Owner's compensation			165	0.5	407	1.5
Total operating expenses			4,087	13.1	3,281	11.9
Net profit (loss)			**2,340**	**7.5**	**2,986**	**10.9**

Figure 6.2. Production builders with land costs: cost of sales, expenses, and net profit (% of revenue)

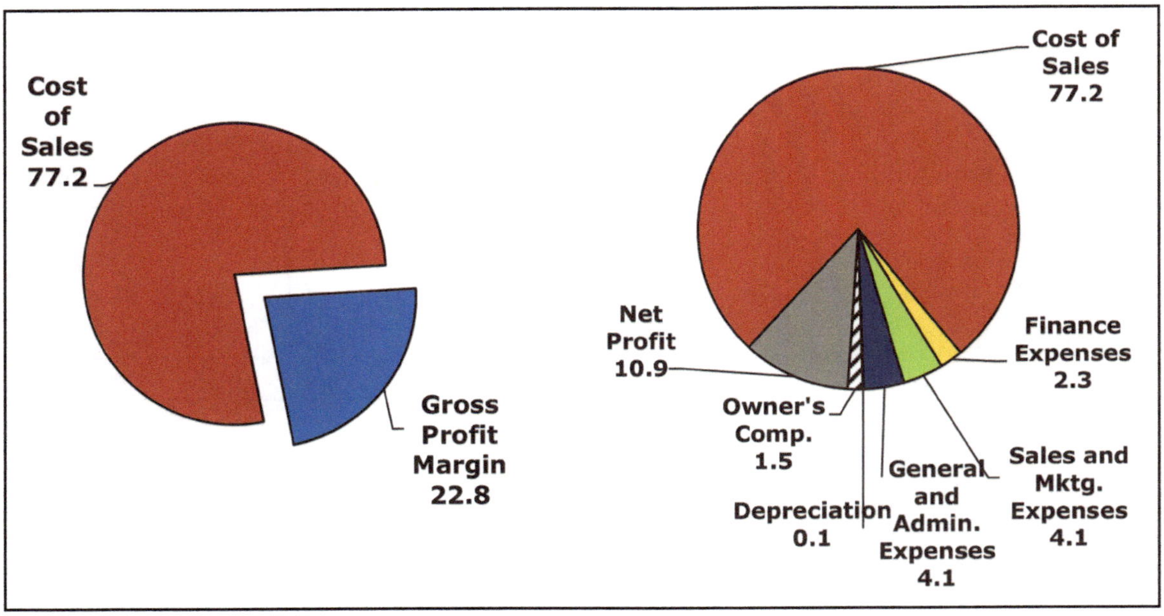

Aggregating balance sheets for all production builders with land costs who responded to the survey shows this group of builders averaged $16.8 million in total assets, about 4% lower than in 2020 ($17.6 million), and in fact, the smallest balance sheet these builders have reported since records began in 2002. One important change between 2020 and 2023 was a relative shift in the type of assets held: the share of current assets fell from 90.1% to 83.5% while the share of fixed assets rose from 9.9% to 16.5% (Table 6.7).

The other side of the ledger shows a change in how assets were paid. Between 2020 and 2023, the total amount production builders with land costs owed to others declined from an average of $12.1 million to $10.1 million — a 17% reduction in debt. At the same time, their average invested capital increased from $5.5 million to $6.8 million — a 24% jump. The changes indicate substantial deleveraging by this group of builders and a larger role for equity as a source of financing. Equity financed 40.3% of this group's assets in 2023, up from 31.2% in 2020 (Table 6.7).

Table 6.7. Production builders with land costs: balance sheet

	2017		2020		2023	
	Average ($1,000s)	Share of total (%)	Average ($1,000s)	Share of total (%)	Average ($1,000s)	Share of total (%)
Assets						
Current assets						
Cash	N/A		2,239	12.7	1,935	11.5
Receivables and inventories			828	4.7	1,044	6.2
Construction work in progress			12,331	70.0	9,928	58.9
Other current assets			477	2.7	1,162	6.9
Total current assets			15,874	90.1	14,068	83.5
Other assets			1,742	9.9	2,780	16.5
Total assets			**17,616**	**100.0**	**16,849**	**100.0**
Liabilities						
Current liabilities			6,075	34.5	1,171	6.9
Construction loans payable			3,642	20.7	5,151	30.6
Total current liabilities			9,717	55.2	6,322	37.5
Long-term loans payable			2,262	12.8	1,407	8.4
Other long-term liabilities			136	0.8	2,326	13.8
Total liabilities			**12,116**	**68.8**	**10,055**	**59.7**
Owner's equity			**5,500**	**31.2**	**6,793**	**40.3**
Total liabilities & owner's equity			**17,616**	**100.0**	**16,849**	**100.0**

Achieving higher returns with lower levels of debt had a positive impact on the group's financial ratios. The current ratio rose from 1.55 in 2020 to 2.23 in 2023, indicating increased ability to pay short-term debts using short-term assets. The debt-to-equity ratio, meanwhile, dropped from 2.18 to 1.48, signaling lower levels of financial risk. Finally, production builders with land costs proved more successful at converting their assets and equity into profits: ROA rose from 13.3% in 2020 to 17.7% in 2023, while ROE increased from 42.6% to 44.0% during this period (Table 6.8).

Table 6.8. Production builders with land costs: financial ratios

	2017	2020	2023
Current ratio	N/A	1.55	2.23
Debt-to-equity ratio		2.18	1.48
Return on assets (%)		13.30	17.70
Return on equity (%)		42.60	44.00

Note: No results were produced for production builders without land costs or production combination builders because of insufficient sample size

7

Builder Financial Performance by Region and Business Model

Single-family home building was by far the primary source of revenue for builders responding to this edition of *The Cost of Doing Business Study,* originating 91.1% of the average $11.3 million they earned in 2023. Residential remodeling accounted for only 3.7% of that revenue, followed by 1.2% from multifamily building, and 4.0% from all other sources combined.

Revenue and Profits by Region

Builders in the West and South regions of the U.S. reported earning over 90% of their 2023 revenue from single-family home building. In the West, 93.3% of revenue came from that single source, about the same share as in the South, 93.0%. Builders in the Midwest had slightly more diversified companies, with 84.8% of revenue coming from single-family home building and another 7.0% stemming from residential remodeling. A breakdown of the income statement cannot be produced for the Northeast because insufficient responses from this region make any estimates statistically unreliable.

Builders in the West spent 6.0% of their 2023 revenue on land costs, a somewhat lower share than builders in the South (8.7%) or Midwest (9.2%). Builders in the West also reported spending 67.4% of all their revenue on direct construction costs for single-family home building (i.e., labor and materials) — the most of any region. In the South, that share was 63.8%, and in the Midwest 61.8%. After accounting for all cost of sales, builders in the South finished 2023 with the highest gross profit margin of any region, at 22.1%, followed by the West (20.4%) and the Midwest (17.9%) (Figure 7.1).

Figure 7.1. Regional differences in costs and profit margins (% of revenue)

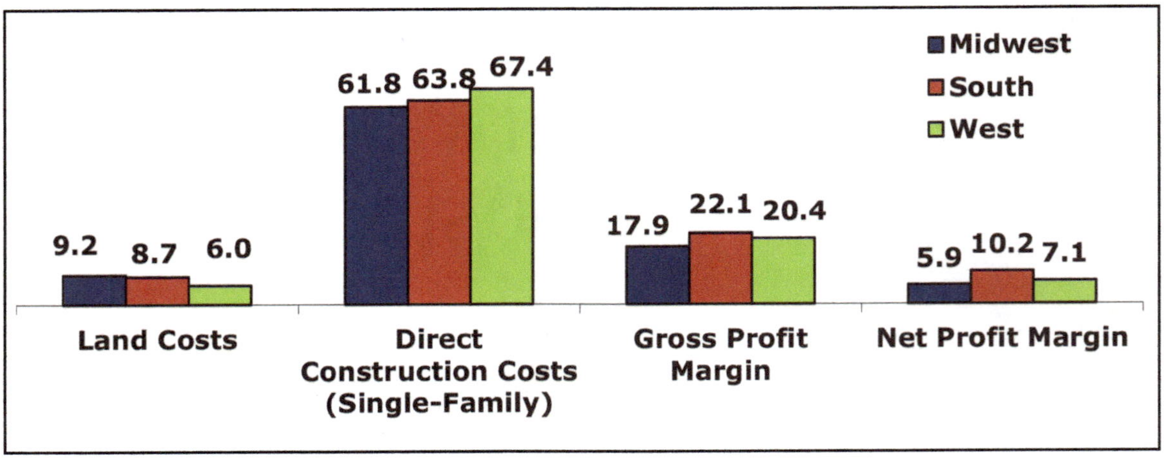

On average, builders in the South spent the smallest proportion of revenue on operating expenses, at 11.9%. Those in the Midwest spent 12.0%, while builders in the West spent the most, at 13.2%. In all three regions, the costliest expense line was general and administrative expenses, which took up 4.9% of revenue in the South, 5.4% in the Midwest, and 7.3% in the West.

After subtracting all expenses from gross profits, builders in the South reported the highest net profit margin of all three regions, at 10.2%. Builders in the West came in second place, at 7.1%, followed by those in the Midwest, at 5.9%.

Quite impressively, Southern builders have been able to consistently improve their bottom line in every iteration of this study since 2010, when they reported an average net profit margin of only 1.7%. Since then, that metric has risen to 3.5% in 2012, 6.1% in 2014, 6.4% in 2017, 7.1% in 2020, and finally to 10.2% in 2023. Builders in the West saw steady increases in their average net margin from 2010 (-2.9%) to 2017 (11.0%), but the metric lost some ground in both 2020 (8.0%) and 2023 (7.1%). Meanwhile, the net margin for builders in the Midwest rose from 2010 (0.9%) to 2014 (7.3%), lost some steam in 2017 (6.7%) and 2020 (5.9%), and remained unchanged in 2023 (5.9%).

Revenue and Profits by Business Model

Historical data for the past five *Cost of Doing Business Studies,* spanning from 2010 to 2023, show that no single business model has won the 'most profitable' title consistently. Builders with land costs, for example, were the most profitable of the three models in 2012 (with a net margin of 6.2%), 2017 (10.3%), and 2023 (10.6%), but the award went to combination builders in 2014 (7.6%) and 2020 (7.2%). Builders without land costs were the most profitable model only once during this period, in 2010 (2.9%).

Figure 7.2 provides further profitability details for each of the three business models for the 2023 fiscal year. Builders with land costs reported an average of $17.9 million in total revenue, of which 77.5% went to pay for cost of sales, leaving them with a gross profit margin of 22.5%. Their owners received compensation equivalent to 1.5% of revenue. Ultimately, this group of builders had the highest net profit margin of the three models, at 10.6%.

For their part, builders without land costs averaged $4.7 million in revenue in 2023, spending 81.3% of it on costs of sales and keeping only 18.7% as gross profit. Owners at these companies received a relatively high share of revenue (4.2%) as compensation. That and other expenses totaling 15.8% of income left them with the lowest net profit margin of the three models, at 3.0%.

Lastly, combination builders averaged $11.5 million in revenue in 2023 and went on to spend 83.4% of it on costs of sales, which left them with a gross profit margin of 16.6%. They paid their owners the smallest share of revenue of the three models, at 1.1%. After accounting for all costs and operating expenses, this group of builders reported an average net profit margin of 7.4%.

Although comparing net profit margins across business models is useful, it may not tell the complete story of profitability. A more comprehensive way to look at a builder's overall performance is to add the company's net profit margin to the share spent on owner's compensation, since there may be little distinction (especially in small companies) between the two items. According to this broader measure of profitability for 2023, production builders with land costs were also the best performers (12.1%), followed by combination builders (8.5%), and then those without land costs (7.2%).

Figure 7.2. Profits and owner's compensation by business model (% of revenue)

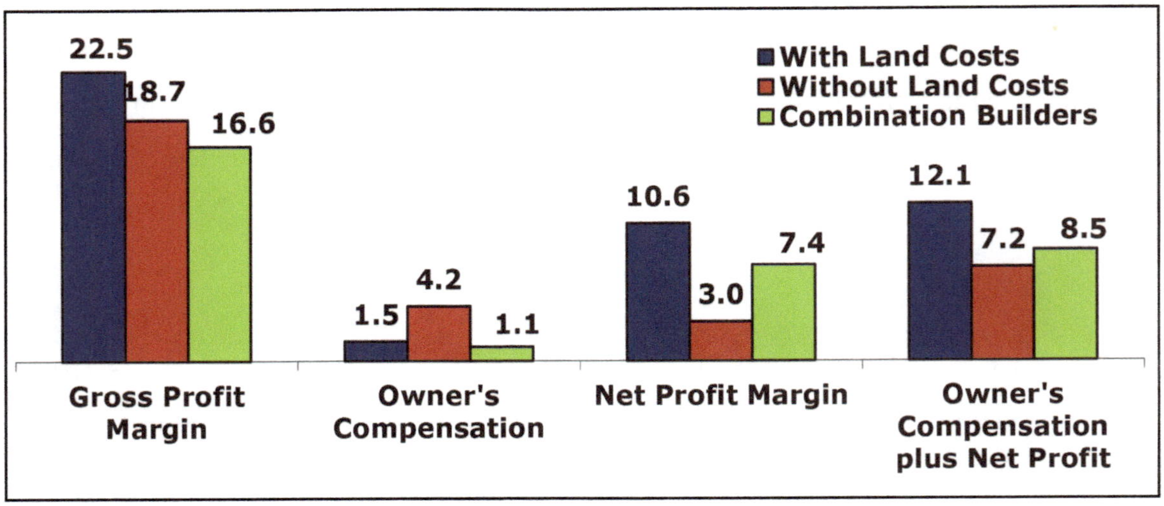

Builders with land costs had the largest balance sheets, with an average of $10.9 million in total assets. Of that amount, $6.3 million was held as construction work in progress (58%) and $1.2 million as cash (11%). Current and long-term liabilities averaged $6.5 million (60% of assets), while owner's equity averaged $4.4 million (40% of assets) (Figure 7.3).

Combination builders followed with an average of $6.9 million in total assets. They held $4.7 million of that as construction work in progress (67%) and another $1.1 million in cash (16%). This group of builders owed $4.3 million (63% of assets) and had equity in their companies worth $2.6 million (37% of all assets).

Of the three business models, builders without land costs had the lowest average assets at \$2.2 million. About \$1.0 million was held as construction work in progress (47%) while another \$578,000 (a hefty 27% share) was in cash. This group of builders reported an average of \$1.7 million in total liabilities (76% of assets) and \$519,000 in equity (24% of assets) (Appendix IV.1).

Figure 7.3. Balance sheet by business model (\$ averages in millions)

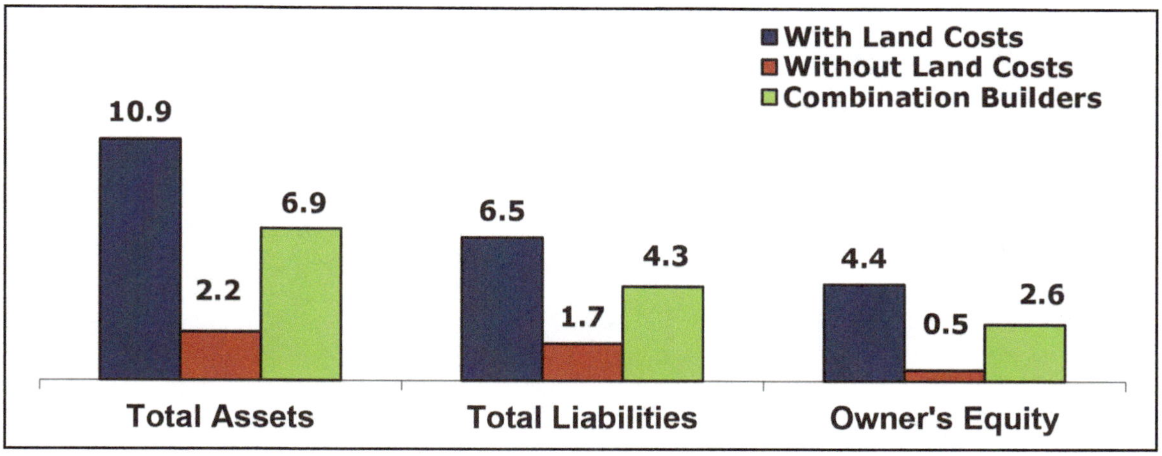

8

Operations

As designed, most respondents to this *Cost of Doing Business Study* — 84% — indicated their primary business activity is single-family home building. More specifically, 38% reported to be single-family custom builders on owners' lots, 27% were single-family production builders, and 19% single-family custom builders on the builder's lots (Figure 8.1). Another 11% of respondents were primarily residential remodelers, 2% were multifamily builders, and 1% were land developers. As stated previously, only respondents whose primary operation was single-family home building were included in the financial analysis presented throughout this report.

Figure 8.1. Main operation (% of respondents)

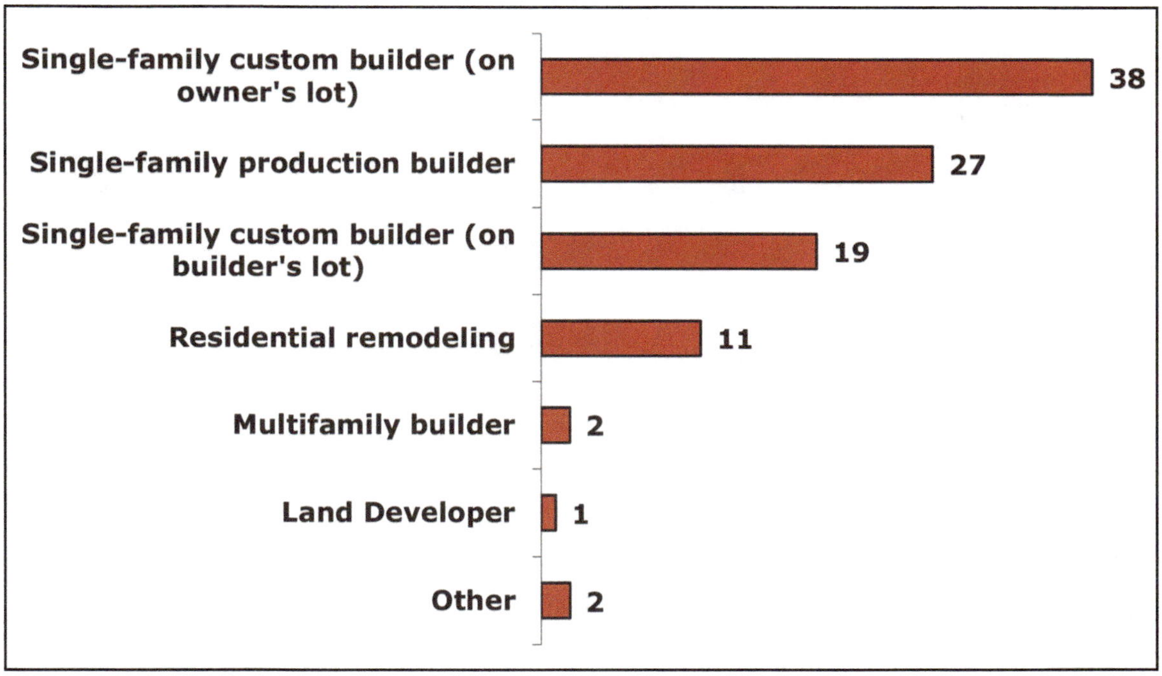

Number of Years in Business

Respondents to the latest *Cost of Doing Business Study* are not new to the industry, having been in business for an average of 27 years. Nineteen percent have been in the residential construction industry for 10 years or less, 20% for 11 to 19 years, 24% for 20 to 29 years, and the remaining 37% for 30 years or longer (Figure 8.2).

Looking at tenure across business models shows that builders with land costs have been in business slightly longer (29 years on average) than builders without land costs (24 years) or combination builders (26 years). Across regions of the country, builders in the Northeast have been in business the longest, for an average of 38 years. Builders in the Midwest average 31 years in business, while those in the South and West average 24 years (Appendix IV.1).

Figure 8.2. Years in the residential construction business (% of respondents)

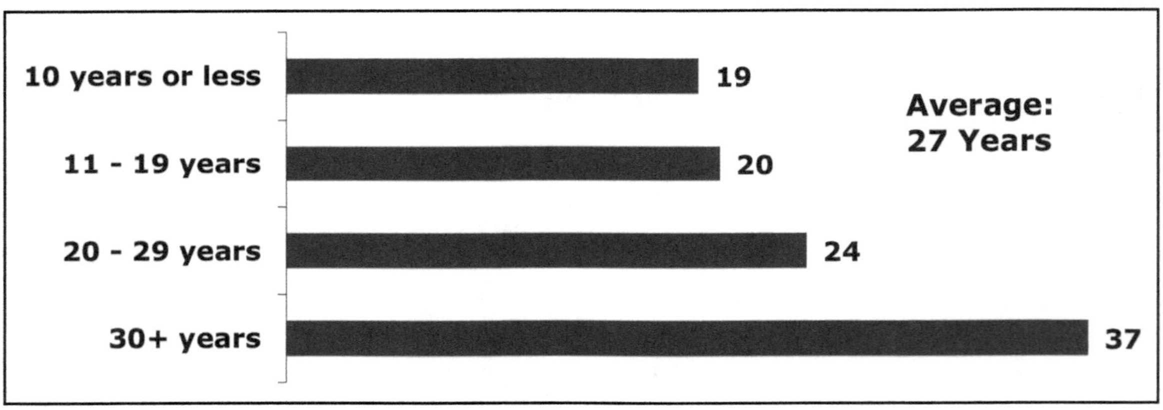

Units Closed: Presold, Speculative, or on Customers' Land

Respondents to *The Cost of Doing Business Study* closed an average of 37 units in 2023. Of those, 12 (32%) were pre-sold on the builders' lots, 13 (35%) were built speculatively (without a buyer at the time of start), and 12 (32%) were built directly on the owner's land (Figure 8.3). Builders' average number of closings in 2023 was higher than in 2008 and 2010 (24 units in both years) as well as in 2020 (26 units), but lower than in 2012 (46 units), 2014 (42 units), or 2017 (38 units). Data from the U.S. Census Bureau on the purpose of construction show that 73% of all single-family units started in 2023 were built for sale (either pre-sold or spec), 13% were built on the owner's land by a contractor, and 6% were built directly by the owner. The remaining 8% were built for rent.

Figure 8.3. Average number of homes closed in 2023 by type of builder

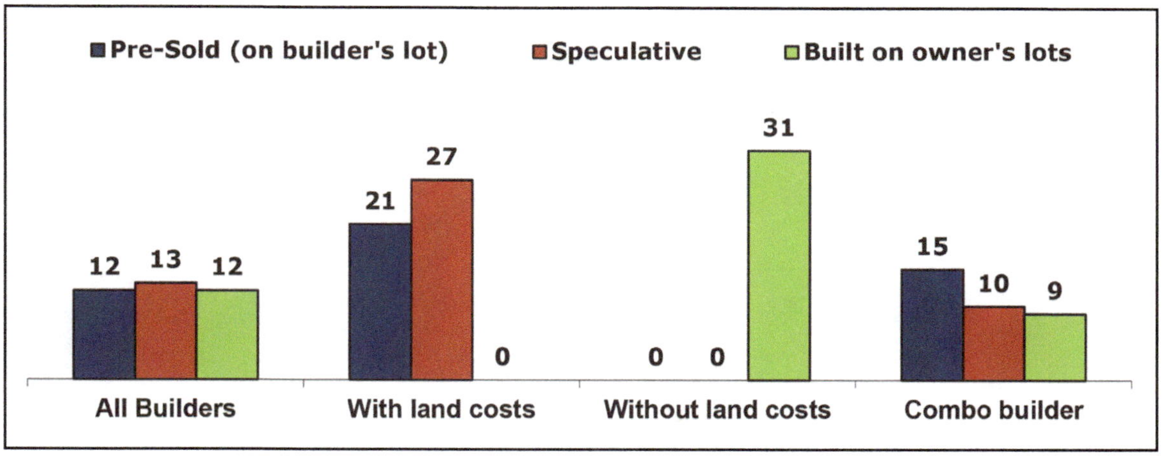

Builders with land costs closed an average of 48 single-family homes in 2023 (21 pre-sold, 27 speculative), a 33% increase from the 36 closings reported in 2020 by this type of builders. Given the small 4% decrease in overall single-family production nationwide between 2020 and 2023 (from 991,000 to 948,000 units started), the increase is likely the result of a shift in the mix of builders responding to the survey in 2023 rather than an actual increase in the levels of production among builders with land costs during this period.

Builders without land costs closed an average of 31 homes on land owned by their customers in 2023, more than four times the seven closings they reported in 2020 and above the 21 closings reported in 2017. There is significant volatility in the number of closings builders without land costs report in each edition of this study, likely due to the composition of the respondents over time.

Combination builders closed on 33 single-family homes in 2023, compared to 26 in 2020 and 45 in 2017. Of the 33 closings, 15 were pre-sold, 10 speculative, and nine were built on the owner's land (rounding of averages may cause the sum not to add up to the total number of closings).

9

Historical Data and Trends

Analysis of historical data from *The Cost of Doing Business Study* reveals that in the 38 years between 1985 and 2023, single-family builders averaged a net profit margin of 5.6%. Their worst financial performance occurred in 2008, the only time in the history of the series when builders averaged a net loss (-3.0%). They barely broke even in 2010 (0.5%), but then returned to healthier net profit margins in 2012 (4.9%), 2014 (6.4%), and 2017 (7.6%). While increased costs and supply chain disruptions during the COVID-19 pandemic caused a mild setback in 2020 (7.0%), net margins rose again in 2023, averaging 8.7% — the highest in more than three decades since the series peak of 10.0% in 1991 (Figure 9.1).

Figure 9.1. Builders' net profit margins (% of revenue)

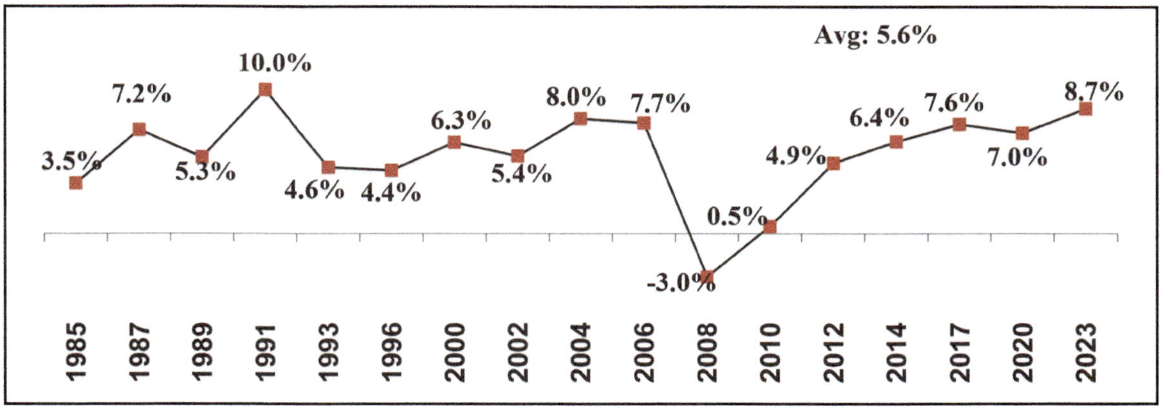

After costs of sales (i.e., land, direct, and indirect construction costs) as a share of total revenue reached a record 85.6% in 2008, builders embarked on focused cost-cutting measures that reduced these costs over the following decade, down to 81.0% by 2017 (Table 9.1). Costs rose slightly in 2020 (81.8%), but resumed their downward trend in 2023, accounting for 79.3% of revenue–their lowest point since 2006 (79.2%).

The gross profit margin for builders responding to the Cost of Doing Business Studies averaged 19.1% between 1985 and 2023. The lowest gross margin happened during the Great Recession in 2008 (14.4%), but as explained in the paragraph above, builders countered the heavy losses that year by curtailing their cost of sales during the following years. That led to their gross profit margin improving steadily from 2010 (15.3%) through 2017 (19.0%), before being pushed back a bit by the pandemic in 2020 (18.2%). Growth returned in 2023, with builders averaging a 20.7% gross profit margin that year, the first time this metric has exceeded 20.0% since 2006 (20.8%) (Figure 9.2).

Figure 9.2. Builders' gross profit margins (% of revenue)

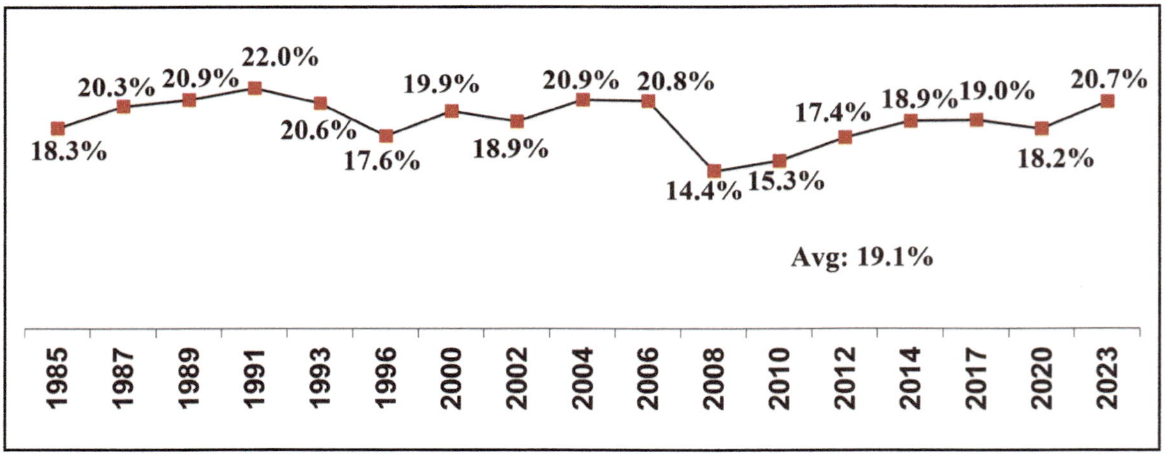

In 2008, operating expenses (i.e., financing, sales/marketing, G&A, depreciation, and owner's compensation) cost builders a staggering 17.4% of revenue. In the following years, they figured out a way to squeeze the fat out of these expenses, reducing them drastically in 2010 (14.7%) and then more slowly through 2020 (11.2%). In 2023, operating expenses shifted higher again, taking up 12.0% of revenue. The increase was mostly the result of higher general and administrative expenses that include salaries, benefits, taxes, and insurance, most of which have seen significant price escalation in recent years (Table 9.1).

Table 9.1 Summary Data from the NAHB Cost of Doing Business Studies (% of revenue)

	Total Sales	Cost of Sales	Gross Profit	Operating Expenses Breakdown					Total Operating Expense	Net Income Before Tax
				Finance	Sales and Marketing	General & Adminis-trative	Depreciation	Owner's Compen-sation		
2023	**100.0%**	**79.3%**	**20.7%**	**1.6%**	**3.1%**	**5.4%**	**0.1%**	**1.9%**	**12.0%**	**8.7%**
2020	100	81.8	18.2	1.3	4.1	4.4	0.1	1.3	11.2	7.0
2017	100	81.0	19.0	1.3	4.7	4.1	0.1	1.2	11.4	7.6
2014	100	81.1	18.9	1.4	5.0	4.7		1.3	12.5	6.4
2012	100	82.6	17.4	1.7	5.1	5.0		0.8	12.5	4.9
2010	100	84.7	15.3	2.1	5.2	5.8		1.6	14.7	0.5
2008	100	85.6	14.4	2.8	5.4	7.5		1.7	17.4	-3.0
2006	100	79.2	20.8	2.5	4.4	5.0		1.3	13.1	7.7
2004	100	79.1	20.9	1.5	4.7	5.4		1.3	12.9	8.0
2002	100	81.1	18.9	0.6	2.6	5.9		4.5	13.6	5.4
2000	100	80.1	19.9	2.2	5.7	3.9		1.8	13.5	6.3
1996	100	82.4	17.6	1.5	3.3	5.0		3.4	13.2	4.4
1993	100	79.4	20.6	1.9	4.0	5.1		5.0	16.0	4.6
1991	100	78.0	22.0	3.0	4.0	5.0			12.0	10.0
1989	100	79.1	20.9	5.6	5.2	4.8			15.6	5.3
1987	100	79.7	20.3	3.3	3.7	6.1			13.1	7.2
1985	100	81.7	18.3	3.9	3.3	7.6			14.8	3.5
1983*	100	79.7	20.3	4.5	3.3	8.8			17.6	2.7
1980*	100	77.2	22.8	2.0	2.5	9.4			16.9	5.9
1978	100	76.1	23.9	2.7	3.6	5.5			16.9	7.0
1975	100	84.1	15.9	2.8	2.3	7.5			11.6	4.3
1970	100	82.4	17.6	3.3	3.0	6.5			14.4	3.2

* The Values for 1980 and 1983 are medians.

Note: The years in this table represent the years the data was collected for, not the years in the book titles.

Source: NAHB

Construction Cost Surveys

In addition to *The Cost of Doing Business* surveys, NAHB periodically conducts a construction cost survey asking builders to break down the costs and expenses of their typical home as follows: finished lot cost, construction costs, financing costs, overhead and general expenses, marketing costs, sales commissions, and profits. The data are national averages because the sample size does not allow for regional breakdowns. Although they are not a perfect tool for estimating the costs of a particular house, the results can provide a broad idea of construction costs for a typical home. Table 9.2 summarizes the results through 2022, the last NAHB survey. A full article on the findings is available on NAHB's website (nahb.org).

Table 9.2 Cost breakdown of a single-family home

	1995	1998	2002	2004	2007	2009
	% of Sales Price					
Finished Lot Cost	24.4	23.6	23.5	26.0	24.5	20.3
Total Construction Cost	53.3	54.8	50.8	51.7	48.1	58.9
Financing Cost	2.0	1.9	2.1	1.8	2.4	1.7
Overhead & General Expenses	5.8	5.7	5.5	5.8	7.0	5.4
Marketing Cost	2.2	1.4	2.4	1.9	2.5	1.4
Sales Commission	3.3	3.4	3.7	3.0	4.3	3.4
Profit	9.1	9.2	12.0	9.8	11.2	8.9
Total	**100.0**	**100.0**	**100.0**	**100.0**	**100.0**	**100.0**
Sales Price	**$183,585**	**$226,680**	**$298,412**	**$373,349**	**$454,906**	**$377,624**

	2011	2013	2015	2017	2019	2022
	% of Sales Price					
Finished Lot Cost	21.7	18.6	18.2	21.5	18.5	17.8
Total Construction Cost	59.3	61.7	61.8	55.6	61.1	60.8
Financing Cost	2.1	1.4	1.3	1.8	1.7	1.9
Overhead & General Expenses	5.2	4.3	5.6	5.1	4.9	5.1
Marketing Cost	1.5	1.1	0.8	1.2	1.0	0.7
Sales Commission	3.3	3.6	3.2	4.1	3.7	3.6
Profit	6.8	9.3	9.0	10.7	9.1	10.1
Total	**100.0**	**100.0**	**100.0**	**100.0**	**100.0**	**100.0**
Sales Price	**$310,619**	**$399,532**	**$468,318**	**$427,892**	**$485,128**	**$644,750**

Source: NAHB Surveys of Builder Members
Note: 2002 data based on survey of builder members carried out in late 2002-early 2003.

According to the 2022 results, about 17.8% of a typical home's sales price pays for the finished lot, which includes raw land and development costs. Construction costs (labor, materials, and subcontractors) account for more than half the price of a home, at 60.8%, while overhead and general expenses take up 5.1%, sales commissions 3.6%, financing costs 1.9%, and marketing costs 0.7%. In the end, an estimated 10.1% of the typical home's sales price goes to pre-tax profits.

When reading the data in Tables 9.1 and 9.2, it is important to keep in mind that results from *The Cost of Doing Business Study* (Table 9.1) are based on company-wide operations, so the percentages are of total revenue spent on expenses from all operations combined. Data from the Construction Cost survey (Table 9.2), on the other hand, are based on builders' estimates of how the price of an individual home is allocated among various categories, so the numbers there represent percentages of an average home's price, not of total company revenue. It is also important to mention that the Construction Cost results shown in Table 9.2 are based on surveys that do not control for the characteristics of the homes sampled, and so the data on prices, square footage, and lot size may change from one survey to the next in ways that do not reflect overall national trends.

Public Firms

The financial reports of publicly traded home building companies offer another view of profitability in the construction industry. Table 9.3 shows revenue and pretax and post-tax profits for the largest 15 public builders (in terms of revenue) for 2017, 2020, and 2023[5]. When aggregated, they earned a total revenue of $149.8 billion in 2023, 46% more than in 2020 ($102.3 billion), and more than twice the revenue in 2017 ($71.4 billion).

All public builders in Table 9.3 posted positive pretax profits for fiscal year 2023. D.R. Horton reported the highest pre-tax profits, at $6.3 billion, followed by Lennar ($5.2 billion) and PulteGroup ($3.4 billion). Altogether, their collective pre-tax profits reached $24.3 billion, 82% higher than in 2020 ($13.4 billion), and 222% higher than 2017 ($7.6 billion). After paying corporate taxes in 2023, their combined total profit was $18.5 billion,

---

[5] Data provided are for each builder's fiscal year, which does not necessarily correspond to the calendar year.

84% higher than in 2020 ($10.1 billion), and an impressive 361% more than in 2017 ($4.0 billion).

Table 9.3. Top 15 publicly traded builders ($ millions)

	2017			2020			2023		
	Revenue	Pretax Profit	After-tax Profit	Revenue	Pretax Profit	After-tax Profit	Revenue	Pretax Profit	After-tax Profit
D.R. Horton	14,091	1,602	1,038	20,311	2,983	2,374	35,460	6,315	4,746
Lennar	12,646	1,190	810	22,489	3,124	2,465	34,233	5,202	3,938
PulteGroup	8,578	939	447	11,036	1,729	1,407	16,062	3,449	2,602
Toll Brothers	5,815	814	535	6,937	587	447	9,995	1,842	1,372
NVR	6,306	847	538	7,537	1,078	901	9,315	1,928	1,592
Taylor Morrison	3,885	739	91	6,129	1,044	243	7,418	1,017	769
KB Homes	4,369	290	181	4,183	364	296	6,411	771	590
Meritage Homes	3,227	248	143	4,482	534	423	6,113	949	739
MDC Holdings	2,578	230	142	3,901	458	368	4,520	526	401
M/I	1,962	120	72	3,046	310	240	4,034	607	465
Dream Finders Homes	--	--	--	1,133	85	65	3,749	404	296
Century Communities	1,423	84	50	3,161	270	206	3,692	351	259
Tri Ponte Homes	2,810	340	188	3,260	373	282	3,715	467	349
Hovnanian Enterprises	2,452	(45)	(332)	2,344	55	51	2,756	256	206
LGI Homes	1,258	171	113	2,368	368	324	2,359	262	199
Total	**71,400**	**7,569**	**4,016**	**102,317**	**13,362**	**10,092**	**149,832**	**24,346**	**18,523**

Under pre-2018 tax law, all businesses could claim operating losses from previous tax years as a deduction against current year net income, thereby reducing current year tax liability. Losses could be carried forward for up to 20 years. Such claims acted to increase after-tax income for accounting purposes by realizing a previously deferred tax asset as income. In other words, the deferred asset, which had potential future value as a future tax deduction, increased after-tax income when realized. The tax deduction reduced taxable income in the year it was carried forward, thus increasing after-tax income by reducing taxes paid.

The Tax Cuts and Jobs Act (TCJA) passed at the end of 2017, however, placed certain limits on the use of net operating losses so that, starting in tax year 2018, businesses may no longer use them to offset all their taxable income in subsequent years. In over-simplified terms, the deduction is now limited to 80% of a business's taxable income, it must be applied in the first tax year in which it has positive taxable income, but may also be carried indefinitely, rather than limited to 20 years. For a more thorough understanding of the impact of the TCJA on businesses, visit NAHB Economics Group's blog (www.EyeOnHousing.org) and look up the tax reform toolkit.

Pre-tax profit margins for the same group of builders are shown in Table 9.4. Aggregately, their annual 10k reports show an average 14.3% pre-tax net profit margin for fiscal year 2023, nearly three percentage points higher than in 2020 (11.5%) and four and a half points higher than in 2017 (9.8%). Only 10 of the builders in Table 9.4 were public companies in 2008, at the start of the Great Recession which became the longest economic downturn in the U.S. since World War II. Collectively, these builders experienced their worst financial performance that year, posting a combined net loss margin of -24.1%.

Table 9.4. Pretax profit margins for top 15 publicly traded builders (%)

	2017	2020	2023
D.R. Horton	11.4	14.7	17.8
Lennar	9.4	13.9	15.2
PulteGroup	10.9	15.7	21.5
Toll Brothers	14.0	8.5	18.4
NVR	13.4	14.3	20.7
Taylor Morrison	19.0	17.0	13.7
KB Homes	6.6	8.7	12.0
Meritage Homes	7.7	11.9	15.5
MDC Holdings	8.9	11.7	11.6
M/I	6.1	10.2	15.0
Dream Finders Homes	--	7.5	10.8
Century Communities	5.9	8.5	9.5
Tri Ponte Homes	12.1	11.4	12.6
Hovnanian Enterprises	-1.8	2.3	9.3
LGI Homes	13.6	15.5	11.1
Average	**9.8**	**11.5**	**14.3**

APPENDIX

I

The 4-Hour Business Plan: A Quick and Effective Budget-Based Plan for Profitability

By Vince Butler, GMB, GMR, CAPS

Business planning is essential to achieving your business goals. Case and point: A builder would never start a project without a complete set of plans, yet most companies enter each year with no formal business plan. They optimistically assume each project will run its course — and the end of the year will find them profitable and financially prepared for the next challenge. However, without a plan, there are no benchmarks to measure progress along the way, which allows a business owner to see if they're ahead or behind their targets. Critical decisions about new equipment, marketing, hiring and selecting projects are made in a vacuum.

Implementing a business plan, provides many benefits for the business owner, including:

- Provide financial benchmarks to control growth and monitor progress.
- Establish target margins and markups needed to achieve goals.
- Focus staff and provide a basis for decision-making.
- Decide where and when to market and evaluate its effectiveness.
- Control cash-flow to keep the business secure.
- Set budgets and control overhead.
- Maximize investment return from the business.
- Higher customer satisfaction.

This article will outline how to create a simple business plan in about four hours. It will attempt to cut through the obstacles that prevent successful business plan development and implementation. A successful plan is a living document that embraces the dynamic, ever-changing environment of the residential construction industry. Keep in mind that the plan must be monitored to work. It must be easy to update and evaluate. Lastly, you must reward the business owner by helping them to take control of their business and achieve their goals.

Goal Setting

The first step to successful business planning is setting goals. Goals are the foundation of a business plan and define why you're in business. Whether we would like to be financially independent, spend more time with family or volunteer at a local charity or climb Mt. Everest, the best method of realizing those goals is to design a business as your vehicle to achieve them. A plan based upon goals means your business success results in a direct personal reward.

To get started, **set short-term goals for the next 12 to 18 months.** List at least five personal and business goals for that period. Confirm your business goals support achieving your personal goals. For instance, if your personal goal is to spend more time coaching your child's sports team, then your business goal should be to limit your work hours allowing you the required time off.

Next, list your personal and business goals for the longer term of 2 to 5 years. Again, be sure to link your business goals with personal goals so the business plan will develop around achieving your personal goals.

It is one of the most important pieces of information at your disposal and without proper understanding, it becomes difficult to know whether your company is struggling or thriving.

All goals should be **SMART: S**pecific, **M**easurable, **A**ction-oriented, **R**ealistic, **T**ime-bound

Review each goal to confirm it is SMART. For example, setting a goal to make your company more profitable is not SMART. The same goal stated correctly: Increase gross profit to 35% by year-end. It is specific (35%), measurable (on the Income Statement), Action-oriented (increase gross profit), realistic (35% G.P. is within industry ranges for remodelers) and time-bound (by year-end).

You will probably notice that most goals have a financial component. If your goal is to climb Mt. Everest, a profitable business will be essential. You will need time away from the business to train and get in excellent physical condition. To do this, the business will need staff to make decisions in your absence. It will require enough money to compensate you even when you are not contributing directly, and it will require systems that increase efficiency and simplify decision-making. All need money and your business goals must recognize this.

The process of goal setting should take about 30 minutes within our 4-hour business plan method.

Budgeting

The next step is budgeting. Don't be intimidated by this task. If you are currently keeping your books using any of the leading business accounting software packages, you're well on your way.

A few key elements are needed to make the budgeting process easier:

1. Confirm your books are set up per the NAHB Chart of Accounts.
2. Confirm you are reporting on an accrual (not cash) method.
3. Produce an Income Statement (Profit & Loss) for last year or the prior 12 months if more than 3 months into the current year.

If your accounts are properly set up, you should be able to quickly create a budget based upon past performance together with your assumptions about the future. NAHB has resources and courses available to learn these accounting concepts, if needed.

A complete budget will include your revenue goals for the coming year, target gross profit margin (GP%), and overhead (including marketing expenses) you expect to incur to produce that revenue and hopefully achieve your goals of owner's compensation and net profit.

The budget process should take about 2½ hours of our 4-hour business plan method.

Contingency Planning

The last hour is spent exploring the "what-ifs." You have set an ideal goal initially but as we know, things don't always work out as planned. To make the plan dynamic and easily adapted to changing conditions we need to consider alternatives. Run the same numbers with a reduced sales volume to see the effect on margins and markups. If sales are lower, overhead will become a higher percentage of gross margin dollars. This requires a higher markup to cover overhead and keep the same net profit goal. Otherwise, net profit will suffer.

Alternatively, consider the effect of exceeding your sales goals. Overhead is now a lower percentage of gross margin, so you could achieve the same net profit with lower markups or create a higher net profit by keeping margins steady. However, you can only increase sales volume an incremental amount before either overhead must increase to manage it profitably or inefficiencies and errors will eat up margins through slippage.

If you reach specific goals throughout the year, continue with planned expenditures. Set thresholds for new investments in equipment and technology upgrades. Identify expenses to postpone if you are behind your sales or margin goals. Decision-making is now grounded in the plan rather than the checkbook.

Monitoring and Performance Evaluation

It is widely accepted that business owners should spend 15–20% of their time on planning. Weekly monitoring of the business plan with bi-weekly or monthly updates and modification will quickly help you achieve the recommended planning time. If your goals are SMART, you will have a measurable metric stated in the goal.

Tracking and Measuring

To monitor the business plan and use benchmarks to gauge progress, it is necessary to have certain tracking systems in place. The income statement will provide revenue numbers, gross profit margins and data on expenses such as sales and marketing as well as total overhead. The "bottom line" is net profit – or the food that feeds the growth of the business. The balance sheet provides a snapshot of the financial condition of a company. It is usually the financial statement a lender looks at first when deciding whether to lend money to a business. The balance sheet provides data on the net worth of the business, how much the owner(s) has at risk, and the return on that investment.

One of the most important metrics for any builder is gross profit. Gross profit is sales less the hard costs of the project. Consider gross profit as the money available to cover overhead and create a profit. In other words, it's what runs the business and rewards the owner(s). Gross profit can be expressed in dollars or as a percentage of sales (margin). Markup is an amount or percentage added to the hard costs that will result in the required gross profit. Understanding the difference is essential to creating a profitable outcome.

Overcoming Obstacles

With this shortened process including only the most essential elements necessary, most builders should be able to implement a basic business plan. But putting it in place and using it is another story. Here are techniques successful firms have used to make the business plan a dynamic part of their management cycle.

Share the plan with staff, business associates, consultants, etc. The more it is shared the more accountable you become. It also creates buy-in from the people essential for its execution. Include your staff in the entire process. Your consultant network (i.e., accountants, lawyers, tax advisors, etc.) can provide essential advice and aid in creating and implementing your plan.

Network with other professionals. NAHB 20 Clubs offer an unparalleled opportunity. By sharing your company's plan with fellow builders, you create accountability. They may have experienced similar challenges before and can share solutions and ideas.

Benchmarking your business against similar companies offers the most accurate way to monitor progress and adjust to changing conditions. 20 Clubs meet twice a year, which means you will revisit and review the plan at least that often.

Establish a regular review process where key personnel are brought together to review the plan and make appropriate changes. If you compare your metrics against the benchmarks you have established you can quickly identify variances. Adjustments can then be made. If the business environment changes or new opportunities arise, the plan can be changed as needed. Similarly, the review process should evaluate all major business decisions to see if they are consistent with the plan.

Now you have the basics of a business plan. It includes a workable and easily modified budget with realistic milestones to control overhead and grow the business while maintaining or even increasing profitability; a marketing budget for realizing your sales revenue goals while protecting your price structure and maximizing profit; and a contingency plan for adapting to changing markets and matching your management decisions with the plan's progress. Hopefully, you will see the benefits of planning and invest more time perfecting your business plan in the future.

Vince Butler, GMR, GMB, CAPS *is a second-generation builder and remodeler from Northern Virginia. He has served as President of Butler Brothers Corporation, a full-service design-build company, since 1984 and has extensive experience in the design, sales and production of residential construction and remodeling.*

Vince is a Graduate Master Remodeler (GMR), Graduate Master Builder (GMB) and Certified Aging-in-Place Specialist (CAPS). He is a nationally recognized speaker on residential construction management topics and an approved NAHB Master Instructor. He has presented at many national and regional trade shows and teaches throughout the U.S. and Canada. He was named NAHB CAPS Educator of the Year in 2012 and Builder Remodeler Educator of the Year in 2017. At the International Builders Show® in 2023 Vince was inducted into the NAHB Remodelers Hall of Fame.

APPENDIX

II

The Importance of Key Financial Ratios and Benchmarks

By David O'Brien

Identifying key financial ratios are a vital component of construction accounting. They provide a more concise picture of a building company's financial health. However, it's important to know that no one ratio can tell a company's complete story — and that's why understanding a variety of ratios is necessary.

Ratios can help identify potential risks, allow owners and shareholders to make more informed decisions and help a company operate more profitably. Having this information is not only helpful to the company, but also to other primary users of the financial statements such as banks and insurance companies.

This course offers a deep dive into calculating and using financial ratios to effectively manage your business. As stated above, different stakeholders rely on key ratios to make decisions about your company including approving a loan or how much bonding capacity to allow. This course will help you understand what ratios these stakeholders use and how to calculate them. Benchmarking, which allows business owners to measure their company's performance against industry standards, will be discussed as well as how to identify potential problems based upon calculated ratios.

Following this course, participants will be able to (1) explain what financial ratios are and why they are crucial in managing a construction business, (2) calculate key liquidity, profitability, and leverage activity ratios, (3) use financial ratios to make better business decisions and (4) prepare a dashboard of key performance indicators or KPIs.

Understanding the Home Builder/Remodeler Balance Sheet

A balance sheet is more than just a financial statement that reports assets, liabilities, and equity. If used properly, it's a tool that can help track the performance of your company. When compared to previous balance sheets, it can give you a much better understanding of how your company is performing over time.

A balance sheet can also be used by potential investors to decide whether they want to invest in your business and can allow owners to craft more effective organizational strategies. Understanding your balance sheet is critical to managing your business.

This course aims to give participants an in-depth understanding of all the elements of a balance sheet including the work-in-process (WIP) and completed contract schedules. We hope this empowers participants to become more confident in their interpretation of their balance sheet and enable them to make better decisions.

Following this course, participants will be able to (1) understand how to read and interpret the balance sheet, (2) describe components of the balance sheet and what information each provides and (3) understand the importance of the WIP and Completed Contract schedules and how to tie them back to the financial statements.

Author R. David O'Brien, CPA, CGMA and Partner & Director of Construction Services, graduated from California State University at Chico, California. He worked for large firms in Reno, Nevada, and Toledo, Ohio, before becoming a partner at Mosley Glick O'Brien, Inc.

O'Brien has an extensive background in assurance and accounting with an emphasis in real estate, construction, manufacturing, and distribution. His primary focus is the construction industry, and his clientele industry includes a variety of contractors, such as general contractors, electrical contractors, and flooring contractors. He is also a member of the American Institute of Certified Public Accountants, the Society of Certified Public Accountants in Ohio, Nevada, and Michigan.

APPENDIX

III

2024 Builders' Cost of Doing Business Survey

2024 Builders' Cost of Doing Business Survey

I. FIRM'S PROFILE

1. Indicate your firm's main operation during fiscal year 2023 and write in the percentage of your business each operation represents.

	Main operation (Check ONE only)	Percent of Your Business
Single-family production builder	☐	______ %
Single-family custom builder (on owner's lot)	☐	______ %
Single-family custom builder (on builder's lot)	☐	______ %
Multifamily builder	☐	______ %
Land developer	☐	______ %
Residential remodeling	☐	______ %
Other	☐	______ %
	Total:	**100%**

2. How many years has your firm been in the residential construction business? ________year(s)

3. Of the total number of single family-units your firm closed in fiscal year 2023, how many were pre-sold, speculative, and/or built on others' land (owners' lots)?
(If none in a category, please write zero.)

	Single-Family Units Closed
Pre-sold (on builder's lot)	________
Speculative	________
Built on others' land (owners' lots)	________
TOTAL	________

II. FINANCIAL INFORMATION

4. Balance Sheet for fiscal year 2023.

Each code number refers to the NAHB Chart of Accounts, found at www.nahb.org/chart]			
Assets		**Liabilities and Owner's Equity**	
Cash [1000-1090]	$	Current Liabilities [2000-2490]	$
Receivables and Inventories [1200-1390]	$	Construction Loans Payable [2230]	$
Construction Work in Progress [1400-1490]	$	Long-term Loans Payable [2510, 2530]	$
Other Current Assets [1500-1690]	$	Other Long-Term Liabilities [2600-2890]	
Other Assets [1700-1990]	$	Owner's Equity [2900-2990]	$
Total Assets	$	Total Liabilities and Owner's Equity	$

Note: Total assets must equal the total of liabilities plus owner's equity.

5. Income Statement for fiscal year 2023.

*Each code number refers to the NAHB Chart of Accounts, found at www.nahb.org/chart		
Revenue from Operations		
Single-family Home Building [3100-3125]	$	
Residential Remodeling Revenue [3130]	$	
Multifamily Revenue [3140]	$	
Light Commercial/Industrial Revenue [3150]	$	
All Other Revenue [3000, 3050, 3160-3490]	$	
Total Company Revenue [sum of the previous five entries]		$
Cost of Sales		
Land Costs [3550]	$	
Single-family Home Building Direct Construction Costs [3600, 3610, 3620,3625] (permits, labor with burden, trade contractors, material costs, other unit-specific construction cost)	$	
Residential Remodeling Direct Construction Cost [3800-3899]	$	
Multifamily Direct Construction Costs [3640]	$	
Light Commercial/Industrial Direct Construction Costs [3650]	$	
Indirect Construction Costs [4000-4990] (job site and non-unit specific construction costs; include job supervision, estimating, purchasing and design personnel, warranty costs, construction vehicles, tools, and any other indirect costs)	$	
All Other Cost of Goods Sold (cost of sales related to items that fall under "All Other Revenue")	$	
Total Company Cost of Sales [sum of previous seven entries]		$
Gross Profit		
Total Company Revenue less Total Company Cost of Sales		$
Operating Expenses		
Financing Expenses [5000-5990] (points and interest on all loans)	$	
Sales and Marketing Expenses [6000-6990] (commissions, sales salaries and burden, advertising and sales promotion, and model home maintenance)	$	
General and Administrative Expenses [8000-8790; 8900-8990] (salaries, payroll taxes, and benefits of non job-related personnel; office & computer expenses, vehicles, travel, entertainment, taxes, insurance, professional services) (exclude owner's compensation)	$	
Depreciation [8800-8890]	$	
Owner's Compensation [8010] (owner's salary, draws, bonuses and benefits)	$	
Total Operating Expenses [sum of previous five entries]		$
Net Income Before Taxes [total company gross profit minus total operating expenses]		$

APPENDIX
IV

Detailed Tables

Appendix IV

IV.1. Cost of Doing Business Study detailed tables

Q1. Indicate your Firm's Main Operation During Fiscal Year 2023
(Percent of Respondents)

	Total	Region				Total 2023 Revenue ($ millions)			Number of Homes Closed				Type of Builder		
		Northeast	Midwest	South	West	<2	2-9.9	≥10	<10	10-25	26-99	≥100	With land costs	Without land costs	Combination
Single-family production builder	27	11	24	31	24	25	17	62	13	28	75	42	58	5	24
Single-family custom builder (on owner's lot)	38	33	38	36	45	58	50	29	64	39	8	42	15	94	38
Single-family custom builder (on builder's lot)	19	33	18	20	9	17	33	10	23	33	17	16	27	2	38
Multifamily builder	2	3	1	2	6										
Land developer	1			2	1										
Residential remodeling	11	14	16	8	12										
Other	2	6	3	1	2										

Q1b. Percent of your business from each operation
(Average Share)

	Total	Region				Total 2023 Revenue ($ millions)			Number of Homes Closed				Type of Builder		
		Northeast	Midwest	South	West	<2	2-9.9	≥10	<10	10-25	26-99	≥100	With land costs	Without land costs	Combination
Single-family production builder	24	9	23	28	21	22	24	51	14	24	57	35	48	6	21
Single-family custom builder (on owner's lot)	33	27	35	32	38	39	44	18	49	35	12	36	12	74	34
Single-family custom builder (on builder's lot)	17	34	16	18	9	24	14	15	23	29	14	16	26	2	35
Multifamily builder	4	6	2	3	8	0	0	6	1	3	5	4	5	1	2
Land developer	4	2	2	5	4	2	1	5	2	4	10	3	5	0	4
Residential remodeling	15	16	19	12	16	14	15	5	11	4	2	7	4	16	3
Other	3	5	3	2	4	0	1	0	1	1	0	0	0	1	1

IV.1. Cost of Doing Business Study detailed tables *(continued)*

Q2. Years Firm Has Been in Residential Construction Business
(Percent of Respondents)

	Total	Region				Total 2023 Revenue ($ millions)			Number of Homes Closed				Type of Builder		
		Northeast	Midwest	South	West	<2	2-9.9	≥10	<10	10-25	26-99	≥100	With land costs	Without land costs	Combination
Under 5 years	5		4	5	8	25	4		8	3	6	1	6	5	5
5-10 years	14	7	11	15	16	17	46	5	18	7	6	14	9	15	15
11-19 years	20	11	10	25	20	8	25	38	16	28	19	20	18	20	22
20-29 years	24	7	26	24	28	33	8	19	26	22	17	29	23	31	19
30+ Years	37	74	49	30	28	17	17	38	32	39	53	36	44	29	38
Average (Years)	27	38	31	24	24	20	18	26	25	27	31	28	29	24	26
Median (Years)	23	38	29	20	20	17	11	22	21	24	31	24	25	21	24

Q3. Of single-family units closed in 2023, indicate how many were pre-sold, speculative, and/or built on other's (owner's) land?
(Average number of homes closed)

	Total	Region				Total 2023 Revenue ($ millions)			Number of Homes Closed				Type of Builder		
		Northeast	Midwest	South	West	<2	2-9.9	≥10	<10	10-25	26-99	≥100	With land costs	Without land costs	Combination
Pre-Sold - on builder's lot	12	14	9	15	8	0	2	19	1	6	21	35	21	0	15
Speculative	13	5	9	18	7	2	6	36	1	5	21	39	27	0	10
Built on other's land -owner's lot	12	13	10	12	12	26	14	5	2	5	4	42	0	31	9
Total	37	33	29	45	27	28	22	60	4	16	47	116	48	31	33

IV.1. Cost of Doing Business Study detailed tables *(continued)*

Q4. Balance Sheet
(Average in $1,000s)

	Total	Region				Total 2023 Revenue ($ millions)			Number of Homes Closed				Type of Builder		
		Northeast	Midwest	South	West	<2	2-9.9	≥10	<10	10-25	26-99	≥100	With land costs	Without land costs	Combination
ASSETS															
Cash	929		617	1,215	710	59	522	1,747	283	1,468	1,280	1,751	1,209	578	1,132
Receivables and Inventories	494		289	552	681	151	222	497	321	451	592	874	806	234	397
Construction Work in Progress	4,428		4,132	4,750	3,875	165	798	9,258	677	3,316	9,132	5,948	6,320	1,018	4,666
Other Current Assets	460		287	505	585	90	189	1,157	141	590	522	1,124	764	173	427
Other Assets	913		460	1,375	476	94	321	1,490	195	318	608	3,367	1,804	177	306
Total Assets	7,224		5,785	8,398	6,327	558	2,052	14,149	1,618	6,142	12,134	13,065	10,903	2,180	6,928
LIABILITIES															
Current Liabilities	1,150		1,162	1,033	1,069	107	310	2,782	265	3,233	1,174	1,101	787	1,029	1,715
Construction Loans Payable	2,049		1,923	2,727	978	100	558	4,464	315	1,157	4,499	2,718	3,410	29	1,985
Long-term Loans Payable	492		50	417	1,258	37	218	626	49	360	1,348	645	910	89	453
Other Long-Term Liabilities	789		17	1,199	863	31	81	617	400	254	136	3,172	1,430	514	189
Owner's Equity	2,745		2,633	3,021	2,159	283	884	5,659	588	1,138	4,976	5,429	4,366	519	2,586
Total Liabilities and Owner's Equity	7,224		5,785	8,398	6,327	558	2,052	14,149	1,618	6,142	12,134	13,065	10,903	2,180	6,928

IV.1. Cost of Doing Business Study detailed tables *(continued)*

Q5. Income Statement

(Average in $1,000s)

	Total	Region				Total 2023 Revenue ($ millions)			Number of Homes Closed				Type of Builder		
		Northeast	Midwest	South	West	<2	2-9.9	≥10	<10	10-25	26-99	≥100	With land costs	Without land costs	Combination
Revenue															
Single-Family home building	10,322		9,866	11,457	7,658	1,019	4,318	22,501	2,718	9,023	20,173	16,775	16,553	3,891	10,741
Residential Remodeling	415		817	200	534	191	401	560	444	340	541	293	0	713	661
Multifamily home building	131		535	0	0	0	0	356	0	0	0	680	325	0	0
Light Commercial/Industrial	12		5	19	0	6	23	1	28	2	0	0	0	25	7
All Other Revenue	447		406	638	12	3	36	1,169	31	86	535	1,579	1,024	55	57
Total Company Revenue	11,327		11,629	12,314	8,203	1,219	4,778	24,588	3,221	9,451	21,250	19,328	17,903	4,685	11,466
Cost of Sales															
Land Costs	946		1,070	1,071	492	75	205	2,289	107	444	1,784	2,288	2,003	0	711
Single-family home building Direct Construction Costs	7,254		7,185	7,856	5,527	774	3,161	15,635	2,157	6,763	14,697	10,284	10,908	3,270	7,945
Residential Remodeling Direct Construction Costs	284		641	148	249	121	251	414	254	287	454	157	0	435	559
Multifamily Direct Construction Costs	91		370	0	0	0	0	247	0	0	0	471	225	0	0
Light Commercial/Industrial Direct Construction Costs	19		4	34	0	5	18	28	21	53	0	0	0	20	56
Indirect Construction Costs	338		238	439	183	47	165	702	121	93	469	896	657	68	237
All other Cost of Goods Sold	52		42	49	82	2	62	69	23	79	66	69	86	14	58
Total Company Cost of Sales	8,983		9,551	9,597	6,533	1,025	3,862	19,384	2,682	7,718	17,470	14,165	13,880	3,808	9,566
Gross Profit	**2,344**		**2,078**	**2,717**	**1,671**	**194**	**916**	**5,204**	**538**	**1,733**	**3,780**	**5,162**	**4,023**	**877**	**1,900**
Operating Expenses															
Financing Expenses	176		194	227	45	20	45	416	16	83	373	390	408	3	52
Sales and Marketing Expenses	349		339	394	221	12	91	836	60	159	835	615	701	94	147
General and Administrative Expenses	608		634	609	598	86	343	1,210	209	810	728	1,111	742	428	705
Depreciation	14		20	11	17	2	9	27	6	29	20	9	14	16	12
Owner's Compensation	211		203	226	205	57	124	398	117	246	209	374	262	198	130
Total Operating Expenses	1,358		1,390	1,467	1,086	176	612	2,887	408	1,326	2,164	2,498	2,128	738	1,046
Net Income Before Taxes	**985**		**688**	**1,250**	**584**	**17**	**304**	**2,318**	**130**	**406**	**1,616**	**2,664**	**1,895**	**139**	**854**

IV.1. Cost of Doing Business Study detailed tables *(continued)*

Q5. Income Statement

(% Share of Revenue)

	Total	Region				Total 2023 Revenue ($ millions)			Number of Homes Closed				Type of Builder		
		Northeast	Midwest	South	West	<2	2-9.9	≥10	<10	10-25	26-99	≥100	With land costs	Without land costs	Combination
Revenue															
Single-Family home building	91.1		84.8	93.0	93.3	83.6	90.4	91.5	84.4	95.5	94.9	86.8	92.5	83.1	93.7
Residential Remodeling	3.7		7.0	1.6	6.5	15.7	8.4	2.3	13.8	3.6	2.5	1.5	0.0	15.2	5.8
Multifamily home building	1.2		4.6	0.0	0.0	0.0	0.0	1.4	0.0	0.0	0.0	3.5	1.8	0.0	0.0
Light Commercial/Industrial	0.1		0.0	0.2	0.0	0.5	0.5	0.0	0.9	0.0	0.0	0.0	0.0	0.5	0.1
All Other Revenue	3.9		3.5	5.2	0.1	0.3	0.8	4.8	1.0	0.9	2.5	8.2	5.7	1.2	0.5
Total Company Revenue	100.0		100.0	100.0	100.0	100.0	100.0	100.0	100.0	100.0	100.0	100.0	100.0	100.0	100.0
Cost of Sales															
Land Costs	8.3		9.2	8.7	6.0	6.2	4.3	9.3	3.3	4.7	8.4	11.8	11.2	0.0	6.2
Single-family home building Direct Construction Costs	64.0		61.8	63.8	67.4	63.5	66.2	63.6	67.0	71.6	69.2	53.2	60.9	69.8	69.3
Residential Remodeling Direct Construction Costs	2.5		5.5	1.2	3.0	10.0	5.2	1.7	7.9	3.0	2.1	0.8	0.0	9.3	4.9
Multifamily Direct Construction Costs	0.8		3.2	0.0	0.0	0.0	0.0	1.0	0.0	0.0	0.0	2.4	1.3	0.0	0.0
Light Commercial/Industrial Direct Construction Costs	0.2		0.0	0.3	0.0	0.4	0.4	0.1	0.7	0.6	0.0	0.0	0.0	0.4	0.5
Indirect Construction Costs	3.0		2.0	3.6	2.2	3.9	3.5	2.9	3.7	1.0	2.2	4.6	3.7	1.5	2.1
All other Cost of Goods Sold	0.5		0.4	0.4	1.0	0.1	1.3	0.3	0.7	0.8	0.3	0.4	0.5	0.3	0.5
Total Company Cost of Sales	79.3		82.1	77.9	79.6	84.1	80.8	78.8	83.3	81.7	82.2	73.3	77.5	81.3	83.4
Gross Profit	**20.7**		**17.9**	**22.1**	**20.4**	**15.9**	**19.2**	**21.2**	**16.7**	**18.3**	**17.8**	**26.7**	**22.5**	**18.7**	**16.6**
Operating Expenses															
Financing Expenses	1.6		1.7	1.8	0.5	1.6	0.9	1.7	0.5	0.9	1.8	2.0	2.3	0.1	0.5
Sales and Marketing Expenses	3.1		2.9	3.2	2.7	1.0	1.9	3.4	1.9	1.7	3.9	3.2	3.9	2.0	1.3
General and Administrative Expenses	5.4		5.4	4.9	7.3	7.0	7.2	4.9	6.5	8.6	3.4	5.7	4.1	9.1	6.1
Depreciation	0.1		0.2	0.1	0.2	0.2	0.2	0.1	0.2	0.3	0.1	0.0	0.1	0.3	0.1
Owner's Compensation	1.9		1.7	1.8	2.5	4.6	2.6	1.6	3.6	2.6	1.0	1.9	1.5	4.2	1.1
Total Operating Expenses	12.0		12.0	11.9	13.2	14.4	12.8	11.7	12.7	14.0	10.2	12.9	11.9	15.8	9.1
Net Income Before Taxes	**8.7**		**5.9**	**10.2**	**7.1**	**1.4**	**6.4**	**9.4**	**4.1**	**4.3**	**7.6**	**13.8**	**10.6**	**3.0**	**7.4**

IV.2. All single-family builders

Top 25% and bottom 25% by net profit margin
Income statement
(average in $1,000s)

	ALL	Top 25%	Bottom 25%
Revenue			
Single-Family home building	10,322	14,978	4,890
Residential Remodeling	415	159	609
Multifamily	131	0	0
Light Commercial/Industrial	12	0	2
All Other Revenue	447	468	484
Total Revenue	11,327	15,606	5,985
Costs of Sales			
Land Costs	946	1,665	321
Single-family home building Direct Construction Costs	7,254	8,851	3,992
Residential Remodeling Direct Construction Costs	284	98	431
Multifamily Direct Construction Costs	91	0	0
Light Commercial/Industrial Direct Construction Costs	19	0	3
Indirect Construction Costs	338	297	174
All other Costs of Goods Sold	52	62	48
Total Cost of Sales	8,983	10,972	4,969
Gross Profit	**2,344**	**4,634**	**1,015**
Operating Expenses			
Financing Expense	176	185	170
Sales and Marketing Expense	349	500	251
General and Administrative Expense	608	810	451
Depreciation	14	5	20
Owner's Compensation	211	374	211
Total Operating Expenses	1,358	1,874	1,102
Net Income Before Taxes	**985**	**2,760**	**(86)**

IV.2. All single-family builders *(continued)*

Top 25% and bottom 25% by net profit margin
Income statement
(% share of revenue)

	ALL	Top 25%	Bottom 25%
Revenue			
Single-Family home building	91.1	96.0	81.7
Residential Remodeling	3.7	1.0	10.2
Multifamily	1.2	0.0	0.0
Light Commercial/Industrial	0.1	0.0	0.0
All Other Revenue	3.9	3.0	8.1
Total Revenue	100.0	100.0	100.0
Costs of Sales			
Land Costs	8.3	10.7	5.4
Single-faily home building Direct Construction Costs	64.0	56.7	66.7
Residential Remodeling Direct Construction Costs	2.5	0.6	7.2
Multifamily Direct Construction Costs	0.8	0.0	0.0
Light Commercial/Industrial Direct Construction Costs	0.2	0.0	0.0
Indirect Construction Costs	3.0	1.9	2.9
All other Costs of Goods Sold	0.5	0.4	0.8
Total Cost of Sales	79.3	70.3	83.0
Gross Profit	**20.7**	**29.7**	**17.0**
Operating Expenses			
Financing Expense	1.6	1.2	2.8
Sales and Marketing Expense	3.1	3.2	4.2
General and Administrative Expense	5.4	5.2	7.5
Owner's Compensation	1.9	2.4	3.5
Total Operating Expenses	12.0	12.0	18.4
Net Income Before Taxes	**8.7**	**17.7**	**(1.4)**

Balance Sheet
(Average in $1,000s)

	ALL	Top 25%	Bottom 25%
ASSETS			
Cash	929	1,498	510
Receivables and Inventories	494	326	143
Construction Work in Progress	4,428	6,553	2,387
Other Current assets	460	606	141
Other Assets	913	1,644	360
Total Assets	7,224	10,628	3,542
LIABILITIES			
Current Liabilities	1,150	1,657	1,611
Construction Loans Payable	2,049	1,919	1,252
Long-Term Loans Payable	492	369	117
Other Long-Term Liabilities	789	111	43
Owner's Equity	2,745	6,571	519
Total Liabilities and Owner's Equity	7,224	10,628	3,542

IV.3. All single-family builders

Small-volume vs. production builders*

Income statement
(average in $1,000s)

	ALL	Small-Volume	Production
Revenue			
Single-Family home building	10,322	4,758	18,548
Residential Remodeling	415	411	423
Multifamily	131	0	325
Light Commercial/Industrial	12	19	0
All Other Revenue	447	49	1,034
Total Revenue	11,327	5,236	20,331
Costs of Sales			
Land Costs	946	216	2,025
Single-family home building Direct Construction Costs	7,254	3,647	12,586
Residential Remodeling Direct Construction Costs	284	264	312
Multifamily Direct Construction Costs	91	0	225
Light Commercial/Industrial Direct Construction Costs	19	31	0
Indirect Construction Costs	338	112	673
All other Costs of Goods Sold	52	41	68
Total Cost of Sales	8,983	4,312	15,889
Gross Profit	**2,344**	**925**	**4,441**
Operating Expenses			
Financing Expense	176	37	381
Sales and Marketing Expense	349	92	730
General and Administrative Expense	608	403	911
Depreciation	14	14	15
Owner's Compensation	211	159	288
Total Operating Expenses	1,358	705	2,324
Net Income Before Taxes	**985**	**220**	**2,117**

** Small-volume builders closed on 25 or fewer homes in 2023. Production builders closed on 26 or more homes.*

IV.3. All single-family builders *(continued)*

Small-volume vs. production builders*

Income statement
(% share of revenue)

	ALL	Small-Volume	Production
Revenue			
Single-Family home building	91.1	90.9	91.2
Residential Remodeling	3.7	7.8	2.1
Multifamily	1.2	0.0	1.6
Light Commercial/Industrial	0.1	0.4	0.0
All Other Revenue	3.9	0.9	5.1
Total Revenue	100.0	100.0	100.0
Costs of Sales			
Land Costs	8.3	4.1	10.0
Single-faily home building Direct Construction Costs	64.0	69.7	61.9
Residential Remodeling Direct Construction Costs	2.5	5.1	1.5
Multifamily Direct Construction Costs	0.8	0.0	1.1
Light Commercial/Industrial Direct Construction Costs	0.2	0.6	0.0
Indirect Construction Costs	3.0	2.1	3.3
All other Costs of Goods Sold	0.5	0.8	0.3
Total Cost of Sales	79.3	82.3	78.2
Gross Profit	**20.7**	**17.7**	**21.8**
Operating Expenses			
Financing Expense	1.6	0.7	1.9
Sales and Marketing Expense	3.1	1.8	3.6
General and Administrative Expense	5.4	7.7	4.5
Depreciation	0.1	0.3	0.1
Owner's Compensation	1.9	3.0	1.4
Total Operating Expenses	12.0	13.5	11.4
Net Income Before Taxes	**8.7**	**4.2**	**10.4**

Balance sheet
(average in $1,000s)

	ALL	Small-Volume	Production
ASSETS			
Cash	929	596	1,482
Receivables and Inventories	494	363	713
Construction Work in Progress	4,428	1,382	7,767
Other Current assets	460	259	780
Other Assets	913	236	1,790
Total Assets	7,224	2,836	12,533
LIABILITIES			
Current Liabilities	1,150	1,038	1,143
Construction Loans Payable	2,049	547	3,735
Long-Term Loans Payable	492	131	1,047
Other Long-Term Liabilities	789	383	1,437
Owner's Equity	2,745	736	5,170
Total Liabilities and Owner's Equity	7,224	2,836	12,533

IV.4. Single-family builders with land costs

Small-Volume vs Production Builders*

Income Statement
(Average in $1,000s)

	ALL	Small-Volume	Production
Revenue			
Single-Family home building	16,553		25,294
Residential Remodeling	0		0
Multifamily	325		535
Light Commercial/Industrial	0		0
All Other Revenue	1,024		1,664
Total Revenue	17,903		27,492
Costs of Sales			
Land Costs	2,003		3,054
Single-family home building Direct Construction Costs	10,908		16,677
Residential Remodeling Direct Construction Costs	0		0
Multifamily Direct Construction Costs	225		370
Light Commercial/Industrial Direct Construction Costs	0		0
Indirect Construction Costs	657		1,012
All other Costs of Goods Sold	86		110
Total Cost of Sales	13,880		21,224
Gross Profit	**4,023**		**6,268**
Operating Expenses			
Financing Expense	408		624
Sales and Marketing Expense	701		1,114
General and Administrative Expense	742		1,122
Depreciation	14		15
Owner's Compensation	262		407
Total Operating Expenses	2,128		3,281
Net Income Before Taxes	**1,895**		**2,986**

** Small-volume builders closed on 25 or fewer homes in 2023. Production builders closed on 26 or more homes.*

Note: Results are not available for small-volume buiilders with land costs due to insufficient responses.

IV.4. Single-family builders with land costs *(continued)*

Small-Volume vs Production Builders*

Income Statement

(% share of revenue)

	ALL	Small-Volume	Production
Revenue			
Single-Family home building	92.5		92.0
Residential Remodeling	0.0		0.0
Multifamily	1.8		1.9
Light Commercial/Industrial	0.0		0.0
All Other Revenue	5.7		6.1
Total Revenue	100.0		100.0
Costs of Sales			
Land Costs	11.2		11.1
Single-faily home building Direct Construction Costs	60.9		60.7
Residential Remodeling Direct Construction Costs	0.0		0.0
Multifamily Direct Construction Costs	1.3		1.3
Light Commercial/Industrial Direct Construction Costs	0.0		0.0
Indirect Construction Costs	3.7		3.7
All other Costs of Goods Sold	0.5		0.4
Total Cost of Sales	77.5		77.2
Gross Profit	**22.5**		**22.8**
Operating Expenses			
Financing Expense	2.3		2.3
Sales and Marketing Expense	3.9		4.1
General and Administrative Expense	4.1		4.1
Depreciation	0.1		0.1
Owners Compensation	1.5		1.5
Total Operating Expenses	11.9		11.9
Net Income Before Taxes	**10.6**		**10.9**

Balance Sheet

(Average in $1,000s)

	ALL	Small-Volume	Production
ASSETS			
Cash	1,209	89	1,935
Receivables and Inventories	806	438	1,044
Construction Work in Progress	6,320	745	9,928
Other Current Assets	764	148	1,162
Other Assets	1,804	294	2,780
Total Assets	10,903	1,714	16,849
LIABILITIES			
Current Liabilities	787	195	1,171
Construction Loans Payable	3,410	718	5,151
Long-term Loans Payable	910	143	1,407
Other Long-Term Liabilities	1,430	45	2,326
Owner's Equity	4,366	614	6,793
Total Liabilities and Owner's Equity	10,903	1,714	16,849

IV.5. Single-family builders without land costs

Small-Volume vs Production Builders*

Income Statement
(Average in $1,000s)

	ALL	Small-Volume	Production
Revenue			
Single-Family home building	3,891	4,338	
Residential Remodeling	713.436	775.449	
Multifamily	0	0	
Light Commercial/Industrial	25.351	34.299	
All Other Revenue	55	74	
Total Revenue	4,685	5,222	
Costs of Sales			
Land Costs	0	0	
Single-family home building Direct Construction Costs	3,270	3,684	
Residential Remodeling Direct Construction Costs	435.485	487.739	
Multifamily Direct Construction Costs	0	0	
Light Commercial/Industrial Direct Construction Costs	19.963	27.009	
Indirect Construction Costs	68	72	
All other Costs of Goods Sold	14	18	
Total Cost of Sales	3,808	4,289	
Gross Profit	**877**	**933**	
Operating Expenses			
Financing Expense	3	2	
Sales and Marketing Expense	94	116	
General and Administrative Expense	428	457	
Depreciation	16	21	
Owner's Compensation	198	236	
Total Operating Expenses	738	831	
Net Income Before Taxes	**139**	**102**	

** Small-volume builders closed on 25 or fewer homes in 2023. Production builders closed on 26 or more homes.*
Note: Results are not available for production builders without land costs due to insufficient responses.

IV.5. Single-family builders without land costs *(continued)*

Small-Volume vs Production Builders*
Income Statement
(% share of revenue)

	ALL	Small-Volume	Production
Revenue			
Single-Family home building	83.1	83.1	
Residential Remodeling	15.2	14.8	
Multifamily	0.0	0.0	
Light Commercial/Industrial	0.5	0.7	
All Other Revenue	1.2	1.4	
Total Revenue	100.0	100.0	
Costs of Sales			
Land Costs	0.0	0.0	
Single-faily home building Direct Construction Costs	69.8	70.5	
Residential Remodeling Direct Construction Costs	9.3	9.3	
Multifamily Direct Construction Costs	0.0	0.0	
Light Commercial/Industrial Direct Construction Costs	0.4	0.5	
Indirect Construction Costs	1.5	1.4	
All other Costs of Goods Sold	0.3	0.4	
Total Cost of Sales	81.3	82.1	
Gross Profit	**18.7**	**17.9**	
Operating Expenses			
Financing Expense	0.1	0.0	
Sales and Marketing Expense	2.0	2.2	
General and Administrative Expense	9.1	8.8	
Depreciation	0.3	0.4	
Owners Compensation	4.2	4.5	
Total Operating Expenses	15.8	15.9	
Net Income Before Taxes	**3.0**	**1.9**	

Balance Sheet
(Average in $1,000s)

	ALL	Small-Volume	Production
ASSETS			
Cash	578	687	
Receivables and Inventories	234	279	
Construction Work in Progress	1,018	1,346	
Other Current Assets	173	198	
Other Assets	177	152	
Total Assets	2,180	2,663	
LIABILITIES			
Current Liabilities	1,029	1,309	
Construction Loans Payable	29	30	
Long-term Loans Payable	89	62	
Other Long-Term Liabilities	514	685	
Owner's Equity	519	578	
Total Liabilities and Owner's Equity	2,180	2,663	

IV.6. Combination single-family builders

Small-Volume vs Production Builders*

Balance sheet
(average in $1,000s)

	ALL	Small-Volume	Production
ASSETS			
Cash	1,132	988	
Receivables and Inventories	397	432	
Construction Work in Progress	4,666	2,146	
Other Current Assets	427	489	
Other Assets	306	324	
Total Assets	6,928	4,380	
LIABILITIES			
Current Liabilities	1,715	1,477	
Construction Loans Payable	1,985	1,291	
Long-term Loans Payable	453	244	
Other Long-Term Liabilities	189	214	
Owner's Equity	2,586	1,155	
Total Liabilities and Owner's Equity	6,928	4,380	

** Small-volume builders closed on 25 or fewer homes in 2023. Production builders closed on 26 or more homes.*

Note: Income statement results are not available for small or production combination buiilders due to insufficient responses. Balance sheet results are not available for production combination builders for the same reason.

Glossary

accounts payable. The amount of money a business owes for products and services purchased on credit.

accounts receivable. The amount of money owed to a business for products and services provided on credit.

assets. Property or items of tangible or intangible value such as accounts receivable, prepaid expenses, and organization costs that a business owns.

balance sheet. A report of the financial condition of an institution that lists the assets, liabilities, and owner's equity at a particular date; sometimes called a "statement of financial position."

builders with land costs. Builders who build only on their lots.

builders without land costs. Builders who build exclusively on their customers' land

capital. Money or assets supplied by banks, investors, or business owners. The dollar value of assets contributed to a business.

chart of accounts. A list of all accounts, and their assigned account numbers, used in recording financial transactions.

combination builders. Builders who build both speculative/presold homes on their own land and custom homes on their customers' land.

current assets. Assets that could be used up or converted to cash within the next business operating cycle, usually one year.

current liabilities. Debts that must be paid within the next business operating cycle, usually one year.

current ratio. A liquidity measure indication of a company's ability to meet its current liabilities. The relationship between current assets and current liabilities is calculated by dividing the dollar amount of current assets by the dollar amount of current liabilities.

debt-to-equity ratio. A measure of leverage equal to the amount of long-term debt divided by the amount of equity contributed by owners.

expense. The payments necessary to operate a home-building business. Expenses reduce revenue. See also financing expenses, general expenses, and sales and marketing expenses.

financing expenses. All interest, points, and service charges related to financing construction activities or company purchases; all closing costs, such as points, taxes, fees, and other miscellaneous charges.

financial ratios. Ratios that identify relationships between different classifications in the financial statements to clearly define a company's financial strength, efficiency of operation, and return on investment.

general and administrative expenses. Expenses that cannot be classified into other expense categories, such as training and education, charitable contributions, and trade association dues.

gross profit on sales. Total revenue minus the cost of goods it sold, excluding financing, selling, and administrative expenses.

income statement. A report on business operations showing net income or net loss for a fiscal period; sometimes called a "profit and loss statement."

liabilities. Amounts owed to creditors; the claims of creditors to the business assets.

liquidity. The capacity to turn assets into cash.

leverage. The degree to which a business uses borrowed money to finance its assets.

loans payable. Long-term company liabilities that represent obligations due over a period. Examples include notes payable and mortgages.

net income. The amount of revenue that remains after deducting costs and expenses for a period.

net loss. The amount by which total costs and expenses exceed total revenue.

net sales. The invoice value of sales minus discounts, returns, or allowances.

operating expenses. The cost of transacting normal business operations, excluding the cost of goods sold, interest, and taxes.

owner's compensation. The amount of money an owner would make doing similar work for another company as an employee.

owner's equity. Owner's claims to the assets of the business. Assets minus liabilities.

production builder. A home builder with 26 or more closings per year.

production combination builder. A home builder with 26 or more closings per year; builds speculative/presold homes on his or her land and custom homes on customers' land.

production builder with land costs. A home builder with 26 or more closings per year who builds only on his or her lots.

profit. The amount of revenue remaining after deducting costs and expenses for a period.

return on equity. Reward for the owners' capital investment.

revenue. The amount collected for goods and services provided; sales.

sales and marketing expenses. All expenses associated with selling homes, including advertising expenses, in-house and broker commissions, models, brochures, and signs.

schedule of accounts payable. A list of all creditors in the accounts payable ledger, the balance in each account, and the total amount owed to all creditors.

schedule of accounts receivable. A list of each customer charge, the balance in the customer's account, and the total amount due from all customers.

small-volume builder. A home builder with 25 or fewer closings per year.

small-volume builder with land costs. A home builder with 25 or fewer closings per year who only builds spec or presold homes on lots the builder owns.

small-volume builder without land costs. A home builder with 25 or fewer closings per year that builds only on land the customer owns.

small-volume combination builder. A home builder with 25 or fewer closings per year; builds speculative/presold homes on his or her land and custom homes on customers' land.

working capital. Current assets of a business that can be applied to its current operations; current assets minus current liabilities.